T0075853

Django Standalone Apps

Learn to Develop Reusable
Django Libraries

Ben Lopatin

Apress®

Django Standalone Apps: Learn to Develop Reusable Django Libraries

Ben Lopatin
New York, NY, USA

ISBN-13 (pbk): 978-1-4842-5631-2
https://doi.org/10.1007/978-1-4842-5632-9

ISBN-13 (electronic): 978-1-4842-5632-9

Managing Director, Apress Media LLC: Welmoed Spahr
Acquisitions Editor: Celestin Suresh John
Development Editor: Matthew Moodie
Coordinating Editor: Aditee Mirashi

Cover designed by eStudioCalamar

Cover image designed by Freepik (www.freepik.com)

Distributed to the book trade worldwide by Springer Science+Business Media New York, 233 Spring Street, 6th Floor, New York, NY 10013. Phone 1-800-SPRINGER, fax (201) 348-4505, e-mail orders-ny@springer-sbm.com, or visit www.springeronline.com. Apress Media, LLC is a California LLC and the sole member (owner) is Springer Science + Business Media Finance Inc (SSBM Finance Inc). SSBM Finance Inc is a **Delaware** corporation.

For information on translations, please e-mail rights@apress.com, or visit http://www.apress.com/rights-permissions.

Apress titles may be purchased in bulk for academic, corporate, or promotional use. eBook versions and licenses are also available for most titles. For more information, reference our Print and eBook Bulk Sales web page at http://www.apress.com/bulk-sales.

Any source code or other supplementary material referenced by the author in this book is available to readers on GitHub via the book's product page, located at www.apress.com/978-1-4842-5631-2. For more detailed information, please visit http://www.apress.com/source-code.

Printed on acid-free paper

Table of Contents

About the Author

Ben Lopatin is cofounder and principal consultant at Wellfire Interactive and has been developing with Django since the pre-version 1.0 days. Over that time he has led a variety of CMS and SaaS projects, using numerous standalone apps and releasing a few himself. He writes a newsletter devoted to working with existing production Django apps called "This Old Pony," named after his most recent DjangoCon talk, and he can be reached at https://benlopatin.com.

About the Technical Reviewer

Ahmed Fawzy Gad is a machine learning engineer who received his BSc and MSc in Information Technology. Ahmed is interested in machine/deep learning, computer vision, and Python. He has a number of open source projects at GitHub (github.com/ahmedfgad). He is a machine learning technical reviewer and consultant helping others do their projects. Ahmed has contributed more than 80 written tutorials and articles to a number of blogs including Paperspace, Real Python, KDnuggets, Heartbeat, and Towards Data Science.

Ahmed has authored three books titled *TensorFlow: A Guide to Build Artificial Neural Networks using Python (Labmert 2017)*, *Practical Computer Vision Applications Using Deep Learning with CNNs (Apress, 2018)*, and *Building Android Apps in Python Using Kivy with Android Studio (Apress, 2019)*.

Ahmed is enthusiastic to find new work opprotunities and a chance to start his PhD. You can reach him through LinkedIn (linkedin.com/in/AhmedFGad), Facebook (fb.com/AhmedFGadd), and email (ahmed.f.gad@gmail.com).

Introduction

At 15 years old, the Django web framework is arguably the most popular Python web framework today and one of the most successful open source Python projects ever. Many things and people have contributed to this, and one of them is the architecture of the framework. Django sites, or projects, are made up of several to many "apps," packages that may include everything from database models to forms and HTTP views required to support one particular part of the project. Not only do apps help organize larger web projects, they also make it possible to reuse that functionality by reusing apps across other projects as their own installable Python packages: Django standalone apps.

This book is for Django developers who are either new to writing their own standalone apps or who have written them before but are looking for some common guidance. You don't need to be a Django guru-ninja-wizard-whatever to write standalone apps, but you will need at least moderate familiarity with Django to use this book.

This book is for developers in two categories:

- You have been working with Django for at least a little while and would like to create a standalone app.

- You have written at least one Django standalone app already but there are aspects of creating another or managing your app, from process to corner cases, that you're unsure of.

The book is roughly grouped into four parts.

The first part is geared toward the developer who has not yet written a standalone app and maybe who finds the idea of putting together, and publishing, a Python package a bit daunting (it's not!). What we'll cover in this part is designed to be enough to get you started with a basic but working and publishable standalone app. In the first eight chapters, you'll learn how to structure a standalone app, manage features like templates and migrations, and create a separate installable package.

The second part is a little bit more strategic. Here we're concerned with the concepts around pulling standalone apps out from existing projects. In this situation you seemingly have an advantage since you already have working code written; however, if you want to extract for reuse, you have to identify where to draw the line between likely coupled code in your own project. More challenging is the prospect of not just making a reusable app based on your code, but replacing your original code with your new standalone app. This part deals with those questions, decisions, and some strategies for these real-world situations.

The third part carries forward the topics in Part 1 including how to work through further issues. How do you best deal with app-specific configuration? How can you support multiple versions of Django or Python? Some of the topics here overlap with issues you'll face in any Django project; however, the details of implementing them, and implementing them well in a standalone app, pose different challenges. This is when you'll need to start considering scenarios beyond your own immediate use case, those things you haven't yet had to worry about in your own projects. If the goal of creating a reusable app is to streamline and simplify the process of building Django websites, then here we want to streamline and simplify the process of building and maintaining reusable apps themselves.

The fourth part is about managing a Django standalone app in the wild. How do you ensure you have a good release every time? What's the best way of ensuring a Django version–compatible pipeline? While there is overlap here with managing any software package, Python or otherwise, we'll focus especially on issues and solutions to Django apps.

PART I

Basic Components of a Django App

CHAPTER 1

Defining the scope of a Django standalone app

Every software project is defined by boundaries, whether you have deliberately chosen them or not. In this chapter, we'll begin our adventure with Django standalone apps by exploring the benefits of developing – and sharing – your standalone app, as well as how to consider what other dependencies to bring along and even whether your Django app should be a Django app at all.

Benefits of creating standalone apps

The benefits of creating a Django standalone app are varied, from the altruistic, the egoistic, and the purely practical.

Sharing your work

Presuming that you're planning on publishing your app as an open source package, the first benefit that most people think about is the value of sharing your work with other people. There's a long history of sharing code in the software community (as long as there is a history of hoarding, too!) because in most cases it's a way that other people can benefit from what you've already done without any opportunity losses to you. Unless you think you'd be able to license and sell your Django app, it is unlikely to be a profitable enterprise in and of itself. So given that you're already benefiting yourself from the work that other people have shared freely, why not share back?

© Ben Lopatin 2020
B. Lopatin, *Django Standalone Apps*, https://doi.org/10.1007/978-1-4842-5632-9_1

Improved code quality

Once you start sharing your work, a knock-on effect tends to be improvements in the quality of your app itself. Most people feel a little nervous the first time they share their work publicly as it is now available for everyone to scrutinize. But just knowing that other people will read and/or use your code tends to make you more careful about how you design and develop it. Once enough people are using it, you'll start attracting contributions from other people, whether in the form of bug reports (yes, identifying bugs is a contribution!), bug fixes, feature suggestions, and new features in and of themselves.

Don't repeat yourself

If you're looking for more hard-nosed reasons, it's time to start dwelling on what it means for apps to be "reusable." As a developer, having reusable code is a time saver and risk reducer. You can use what's already been created and what you know already works.

Imagine if every time you created a new Django project you had to write your own authentication system from scratch, including views, middleware, and models. Inevitably you'd probably just end up copying and pasting code from one project to another, hopefully leaving the mistakes behind, and never really having a single collection of best practices to point to. Thankfully you don't have to, because such a reusable app exists in Django's contrib module.

That gets to the point about risk. Risks in your code can range from bugs to important features you hadn't thought of, and, *all things being equal*, these risks increase when you're starting from scratch and on your own. What we're seeking from our reusable apps isn't just time saved from having to write code from scratch, it's also the accretion of best practices, of features contributed from real-world use, and bugs that have had an opportunity to be squashed.

Commonality across a company

For developers and teams supporting a variety of deployed Django apps, supporting a product or variety of products in a single company, for example, extracting common functionality into reusable apps, is a way of ensuring that functionality works as expected everywhere and gives you leverage in fixing bugs or adding critical new features such that this can be deployed with a version update wherever it's used.

Examples include customized user apps, domain-specific models (e.g., health sciences, finance), asset management, and generic utilities.

Commonalities across client projects

For developers and teams in freelancer or agency roles, working with varieties of clients and projects, reusable apps are a way of carrying useful functionality across projects.

Most of the popular content management and ecommerce solutions in Django came about this way. Both Django CMS and Wagtail, two popular Django-based content management systems and also standalone Django apps, were developed by creative agencies as solutions for client projects.

The currency of prestige

Lastly, though usually unspoken, is the perceived prestige - we won't use the word "vanity" - of having a popular or at least useful standalone app. For product teams, agency teams, and freelancers alike, a shared standalone app is a demonstration of competence, opinion, and vision. It can be used to attract potential hires and potential clients.

The aforementioned content management systems, Django CMS and Wagtail, were created by Divio and Torchbox, respectively. They did great work, but how many Django developers would know their names were not for the contribution of their respective CMSs? Their name recognition in hiring is now certainly improved. I can't speak to any special notoriety myself, but several clients have discovered me both directly and indirectly due to Django apps I've published myself.

Now, if this is the only reason you want to create and publish a Django standalone app, I'd gently suggest pointing your attention elsewhere. The knock-on effects of having an app that people use even in large numbers may accrue slowly, and you're unlikely to either enjoy the process of building and maintaining an app, and your user base will probably suffer, too.

But if your goals include sharing with the community, creating ever-improving code libraries, and reducing development time and risk, then the effort's worth it regardless of how many fake Internet points your GitHub profile earns you.

With or without Django?

In defining the scope of a potential Django standalone app, the first questions you need to ask are whether the package you have in mind needs to be a Django app or just a Python package using Django and secondly how Django-specific your package ought to be even if it isn't an app.

The first question is a somewhat minor question, but gets at how your app should be integrated into other Django projects and development workflows. It's easy to see Django imports in your Python files and think "ah, this is an app," when in fact it's non-installable library code (non-installable in the sense of your INSTALLED_APPS, not in the sense of an installed package). For example, if you had some additional form fields that you wanted to distribute, these could be distributed and used as a "regular" Python library, without adding the module to your list of INSTALLED_APPS. You'll still have to consider the issues discussed in subsequent chapters, such as testing (3, 21), documentation (22), and packaging (8), but with minor differences in how you set up your tests and document usage.

On the other hand, your prospective package may be incredibly useful in Django projects but have no hard requirements on Django, being agnostic to web framework or even to being used for web applications at all. If this is the case, then you should head down this road.

Why ensure this separation? For starters, if you're going to be sharing this with the rest of the world, and the core functionality doesn't actually depend on Django, then you've broadened the audience. You're also reducing yet another dependency in your package, which, even if you're using it in Django projects, is another line of dependencies that can break. Where it makes sense, reference the standard library instead of Django utilities. If something moves in a new Django version, you're now insulated from that change.

It's worth keeping in mind that you can add functionality to Django projects without Django-specific modules, or without necessarily requiring Django. In Chapter 16 on mixed dependency support, we'll examine how to separate out what's Django specific and what's not.

Choosing your dependencies

The great thing about packages like the one you're creating is that they give you functionality for free - maybe not free, but without the cost of writing the code and figuring out the edge cases yourself. These benefits presume that the dependencies you're using are tested and work as advertised and that they continue to be supported with new versions of Python, Django, and their own individual dependencies.

Each dependency you add increases the surface area that you need to test as well as opportunities for broken interactions. This is true in a Django project and it's equally true in your own standalone app. Now, it's certainly unwise to rewrite everything yourself! But give careful thought to whether you really need to add each dependency in your project.

Among the guiding questions, you should consider

1. Does the dependency provide necessary functionality for your app?

2. Is it up-to-date with the Django version(s) you will be supporting?

3. What kind of test and documentation coverage does it have?

4. How committed do the maintainers seem?

Necessary functionality

It's easy to add dependencies to projects and libraries alike. In most Django projects, there's one "consumer" of the project, that is, the project team. It could be a large team with several different environment deployments and millions of users, but that team and that app are still the sole consumer. With a reusable library like a Django standalone app, you can expect that it will be used across dozens, maybe thousands, of other projects. Each dependency for your app is a dependency for projects using your app. And each dependency you add to your app is a potential blocker if it contains bugs or incompatible code and exposes you to risks.

That's not significantly different from how you might look at adding dependencies into a Django project; however, it's easier to back out of these changes when you control the end deploy and other people haven't come to depend on your own code.

So ask if it's necessary to add this, not in the strictest logical sense but whether it's adding more than a minor convenience.

This is a "mistake" I've made. An example of this in my own case is a decision to use the otherwise fantastic django-extensions app as a dependency for my own, django-organizations. I wanted a timestamped model – a good thing to have which you'll notice when it is missing – and moreover I wanted slug fields that took care of themselves. For this I wanted the AutoslugField. This wasn't a bad decision so much as a restrictive one. However, I could have used a typical Django slug field, but for my own needs, the Autoslug was where it was at. Later I realized that some people, including myself, might need to be able to configure how slugs are made, and this should not be so fixed.

Version compatibility

Thanks to the end of life of Python 2, the considerations of Python version compatibility are less significant today than they were two or even one year ago. However, Django compatibility is still an issue. Does the dependency in question support the current version of Django that you mostly work with? That's an obvious starting question.

But you'll also want to know whether it supports older versions and whether it looks like there's any effort to support future versions. It's important that any dependencies you add support the same versions of both Python and Django that your app will support.

A good rule of thumb to look for is support for Django's long-term support (LTS) versions.

Testing and documentation

When looking for tests and documentation in a dependency, we're looking for several things:

1. Verification that the code works and that bugs can be tested against

2. Explanations for how to install and use the package, as well as why it exists

3. Signals that someone cares

Certainly you should find tests in the dependency and tests that extensively cover the package's functionality. You should also look for automated test runs using a continuous integration (CI) system, such that you can see that tests are always run when someone pushes code to the repository. It's much harder to trust that someone is just running the tests on their own, and if there is no CI system tied to the repository, then you'll have to trust that contributors are running the tests and that they're passing.

Basic documentation is important to ensure you know how to set up the dependency and what the edge cases might be. For example, what does it do that is unexpected or what related packages is it incompatible with? For larger dependencies, extensive documentation is a must, but for smaller dependencies, documentation is as much a help as it is a signal that the package has a specific mission (use case) and providing sufficient context that you can judge whether the author and/or maintainers have considered and support various use cases and developers beyond their own initial problem.

The third point leads directly to maintenance cadence.

Maintenance cadence

Does it look like this dependency is and will be actively supported? Is there a significant number of unresolved issues, specifically bugs, that have not been addressed? Are there pull requests, especially for bugs, that are outstanding and old? And a more significant question that many people overlook is, even if issues are reported and pull requests merged, do these result in new published releases? If pull requests have been merged over the last year but no new releases have been issued in that time period, it may not be sufficiently maintained.

Specific vs. generalized

As programmers, we have a tendency to build a solution and then see how that solution can be abstracted to solve more problems. This is, arguably, a very good thing. However, it's easy to get carried away and try to cover too much ground, to go down a rabbit hole of making beautiful abstractions instead of "just" solving the concrete problem in front of you.

For example, you might have a subscription management library for SaaS apps which is built with Stripe. A more generalizable approach would account for different subscription and payment backends. However, unless you actively make use of these different scenarios yourself, trying to handle them all is likely to lead to halfway solutions. And creating a more general system capable of handling user-customized scenarios when you start out with your app will cause you to spend more time on abstractions that could be better spent getting your app polished.

Writing your app to cover every use case you can think of is almost certainly a mistake, regardless of how useful the more general case is. You're likely to spend time anticipating nonissues and failing to anticipate actual needs. It's a much better position to add more use cases, or make more general, working solutions, than to build an overly abstract solution that solves no clear problems.

Summary

In this chapter, you learned about the benefits of creating standalone apps, including the opportunity to share solutions to common problems, aiding code quality through open source scrutiny, and improving the development process by standardizing frequently encountered problems. You also learned about differentiating between Django-related Python projects and Django apps and how to weigh the inclusion of additional dependencies. In the next chapter, we'll examine the structure of a standalone app.

CHAPTER 2

Structuring standalone Django apps

Beyond the scope of *functionality* that you include in your standalone Django app, at a more practical level, you'll also need to structure the code for reuse. There's little fundamentally different about the structure of a *standalone* Django app from a Django app embedded directly in your Django project's codebase. However, there are several practices you'll want to follow to maximize the usability of your app. We'll look at those in this chapter.

Django apps as Python modules

Let's reiterate that a Django app, standalone or otherwise, is a Python package. That is, it's made up of multiple Python modules, that is, Python files, and can import from other packages and from which other packages can import as well. What makes a Python package a Django app, specifically, is that it has functionality, classes, and functions that can only be made use of in a Django project by explicitly including them in the project's INSTALLED_APPS list. It's not sufficient that the package exists in your Python path.

You can add any Python package you want to INSTALLED_APPS, but if it's not a Django app, it will do absolutely nothing for you. We can think of a Django app like an interface, or if we had something abstract like base classes (Python's abc module), but for *modules* it would probably look like this:

- The package includes a models package with one or more concrete models.

- The package includes a template tags module containing tag module libraries.

© Ben Lopatin 2020
B. Lopatin, *Django Standalone Apps*, https://doi.org/10.1007/978-1-4842-5632-9_2

- The package includes a templates directory of HTML templates.

- The package includes a static assets directory including images, CSS files, JavaScript files, and many more.

- The package includes management commands, that is, modules within the myapp.management.commands module of your app (myapp) defining a Command class inheriting from django.core. management.BaseCommand

- The package defines a default AppConfig class.

Any of the first five is sufficient to provide functionality that requires having an installed Django app. The last, defining a default AppConfig class, is a best practice, but in and of itself, it doesn't provide much in the way of functionality itself. It does allow you to make changes to basic app configuration and namespace (more on this later).

It is sufficient to match the expected interfaces to provide installable content from your Django app, standalone or otherwise. Knowing that, avoid relying solely on the module interface for your standalone app, even if this works just fine within your own projects. The point of creating a standalone app is to allow for reuse across all kinds of Django projects, and so you should be as explicit as possible.

Historically, the one and only step to ensure a package was identified as a Django app was to include a models module. If you're working under the assumption that this is still the case, it is not. It is not necessary to include a models module unless you are including model classes in your app. If your app consists only of template tags, you can include nothing more than the following, including the __init__.py file for ensuring the directory is a package, the templatetags module for including any and all template tag libraries, and the boo_tags.py file for defining a tag library including template tags and/ or filters which can be loaded into templates using {% load boo_tags %}:

```
boo
|— __init__.py
|— templatetags
|   |— __init__.py
|   |— boo_tags.py
```

Now if you want to make use of the template tag boo from boo_tags, all you need to do is add boo to your INSTALLED_APPS and you can load the tag library anywhere in your project.

The app that contains the custom tags must be in INSTALLED_APPS in order for the {% load %} tag to work. This is a security feature: it allows you to host Python code for many template libraries on a single host machine without enabling access to all of them for every Django installation.[1]

What about middleware and URLs and views?

Many Django apps include additional Django-related features like middleware, views, URL definitions, and context processors. It even suggests so right in the Django documentation:

> Applications include some combination of models, views, templates, template tags, static files, URLs, middleware, among others. They're generally wired into projects with the INSTALLED_APPS setting and optionally with other mechanisms such as URLconfs, the MIDDLEWARE setting, or template inheritance.

These features are beneficial and even necessary for some Django apps, but strictly speaking they do not require a Django app to use. You can include URLs, middleware classes, forms, and even views from any Python package, whether it's a Django app in your INSTALLED_APPS or a Python package available on your path.

A Django library is no less useful just because it's not an installable app. Forms, middleware, and views, for instance, are core components of Django projects. How your library is integrated into other Django projects will differ slightly, but the steps to plan, test, develop, and maintain your library will not differ significantly.

Example app: currency

We'll start with a very basic example app. This is an app to make working with currencies easier. At their base, currencies values are just numeric values, specifically decimal values, that refer to an amount in a specific denomination and often at a specific point in time. About $10 is not the same as €10, and $10 in 2015 dollars is not the same as $10 in 1990 dollars.

---

[1]Django docs: `https://docs.djangoproject.com/en/2.2/howto/custom-template-tags/` `#custom-template-tags-and-filters`

What we want to do is to make it easier to toggle the display of currency amounts and easily format them. To start with, we just want to change the formatting of certain numbers, so we're just adding a couple of template filters.

The question in front of us is this: is it necessarily a Django app? As we build this out, more and more of the functionality may be mostly non-Django specific, but if we're going to add template tags, they necessarily must be part of a Django app. Otherwise, we can't load the tags library. Since this includes a feature that must be accessed from an installed app in INSTALLED_APPS, this will be a Django app.

We'll start out the app, called currency, with just the necessary files at first. The file structure will look like this:

```
currency
|── __init__.py
|── apps.py
|── templatetags
|   |── __init__.py
|   |── currency_tags.py
|── tests.py
```

The currency folder including an **__init__.py** file defines our module. Our core functionality is just template tags and filters for now, so we just have a template tags module, again with the **__init__**.py file and then the tag library name.

There's one tests.py file for our tests and then an apps.py file. In order to satisfy the requirements of a Django app, our package must define a models.py file or an apps.py file, ideally including the latter even with a models.py. This allows us to define things about our app and ensure that it's picked up by Django as an app.

So now let's look at the content. Our __init__.py files are empty (for now).

Here's our apps.py file:

```python
from django.apps import AppConfig

class CurrencyConfig(AppConfig):
    name = "currency"
    verbose_name = "Currency"
```

Here's our tags library in currency_tags.py:

```python
from django import template

register = template.Library()

@register.filter
def accounting(value):
    return "({0})".format(value) if value < 0 else "{0}".format(value)
```

And here's our tests.py file:

```python
import unittest
from currency.templatetags.currency_tags import accounting

class TestTemplateFilters(unittest.TestCase):

        def test_positive_value(self):
            self.assertEqual("10", accounting(10))

        def test_zero_value(self):
            self.assertEqual("0", accounting(0))

        def test_negative_value(self):
            self.assertEqual("(10)", accounting(-10))
```

Summary

In this chapter, you learned what constitutes, and how to structure, a Django app and how to differentiate between a Python package that includes functionality useful to Django projects and one that is necessarily a Django app. In the next chapter, we'll look at tests for your Django app, including their value and how to include them.

CHAPTER 3

Testing

Tests ensure that our code does what we expect it to do. They also ensure that changes to the codebase don't break something unexpected, and they signal to other users of our app that they can depend on the code.

In this chapter, you'll learn exactly how tests provide value in a standalone Django app, how to run your app's tests outside of a Django project, how to test more complicated multi-app relationships, how to include your tests, and also whether or not you need to configure Django in order to test your app.

Why test?

Everyone says that you should test. It sounds obvious - if testing is good, we should do it. But this begs the question about the benefits of testing.

Testing your Django app several purposes. Written in conjunction with, or before your application code, tests helps provide a working specification against which your code can be verified. In this capacity they can also help shape the code and interface, as if you're adding some feature from scratch, a test will give you your first chance of using it.

Once in place, even otherwise trivial tests serve to protect against regressions introduced by seemingly trivial changes to the codebase.

While not their primary use, tests can also provide an example of how to use your code. In this capacity they're certainly not a replacement for proper documentation, but tests as code examples - especially when tests are run automatically - are a form of documentation that you can verify is up to date.

Underlying all of this is the fact that computer programs are written by human beings and we humans are terribly unreliable when it comes to writing reliable code on our own (apologies if this does not apply to you). There are all kinds of things we can't predict, edge cases we're not good at seeing right away, and interactions that aren't obvious at the surface of our code.

© Ben Lopatin 2020
B. Lopatin, *Django Standalone Apps*, https://doi.org/10.1007/978-1-4842-5632-9_3

Testing doesn't solve all of these problems, but tests provide a potent tool to remove a lot of uncertainty about our code. Ultimately tests provide confidence, both for you and other users of your app - and don't forget that "future you" is likely one of those users!

Testing apps from a Django project

Django projects provide a way to run tests with the test management command:

```
python manage.py test
```

This command will run all tests in your Django project. The scope can be narrowed to run only individually namedi apps by using the test management command combined with the app name, like so:

```
python manage.py test myapp
```

So if the very simple myapp looks like this

```
myapp/
    __init__.py
    models.py
    tests.py
```

with a simple tests.py file like so

```
from django.test import TestCase
from myapp.models import SomeModel

class TestSomeModel(TestCase):
        def test_str_method(self):
                instance = SomeModel()
                self.assertEqual(f"{instance}", "<Unnamed Instance>")
```

then the command python manage.py test myapp will run all of the test in myapp. tests using Django's default test runner, for example, with the example tests file given, the command will run the TestSomeModel.test_str_method.

This works just fine when you're working from a larger Django project, for example, if you're developing your app in the context of a working project. It's of much less help if your app is a standalone library where the code is intended to be managed from *outside* of a project. For a standalone app, it'd be much preferable to be able to run tests just like any other Python package.

Testing the app

If you've worked with other Python packages before, you'll have noticed that they're tested in a straightforward way. There'll be a test module somewhere and usually the setup.py file defines a test script to run using the python setup.py test command. That works for packages using Django, too, with the caveat that much Django functionality must be run from the context of a Django project, something Python's unittest won't take care of for you.

To motivate some reasonable ways of testing a standalone app, let's consider the most immediately available strategy for testing the app: testing from whatever project you're using the app in (presuming you are extracting it).

This means that to test the myapp app, it needs to be installed on the same path as your working project, that is, the same virtual environment, and that it needs to be in your working project's INSTALLED_APPS. When it's time to test changes to myapp, you'll need to go back to the working project to run them, that is, running ./manage.py test myapp.

If this sounds less than sensible, you're on the right track. However, this strategy doesn't allow testing a standalone app, which means it's not repeatable for anyone else who isn't working with your project. And if you're going to package the app for reuse, you won't have recourse to your original project. Thankfully there's a better way.

Testing outside of a project

To motivate our subsequent solutions, we'll set up the most obvious solution possible. This will entail setting up a dummy, or holder, project and running the tests from there. To do, we would create new Django project in our app's root folder, parallel to the app source folder itself. This project will then include our app in the INSTALLED_APPS list.

Then, running the tests and any other commands is as simple as invoking the holder project's manage.py file just like any other project.

Next step is to create an example project in the package root that will be a stripped down project only including our app. Now we can run manage.py commands directly in our package and test the app. You might even add a bash script at the project root that will execute the tests no matter where they're located.

```
#!/bin/bash

cd sample_project
python manage.py test myapp
```

Here's what the layout would look like:

```
sample_project
    __init__.py
    settings.py
    url.spy
    wsgi.py
  __init__.py
  manage.py
myapp/
    __init__.py
    models.py
    tests.py
```

Then to run the tests for your app, you'd run them from the example project just as if it were a production-ready Django project:

```
python manage.py test myapp
```

This works and is an improvement over the original example, but it still adds more than necessary just to run our tests.

Using a testing script

Of course, Django doesn't demand that we have project scaffolding, just that Django settings are configured. So a better solution is a Python script that configures those minimalist settings and then runs the tests.

The script needs to do three things:

1. Define or configure Django settings

2. Trigger Django initialization (i.e., with django.setup())

3. Execute the test runner

There are two ways to provide Django settings. One is to configure them directly in a test script with keyword arguments for settings.configure(). The other is to point to a test-only settings.py module, just as you would, running a production app. The following is a small example of the former:

```python
#!/usr/bin/env python

import sys

import django
from django.conf import settings
from django.test.utils import get_runner

if __name__ == "__main__":
    settings.configure(
        DATABASES={"default": {
            "ENGINE": "django.db.backends.sqlite3"
        }},
        ROOT_URLCONF="tests.urls",
        INSTALLED_APPS=[
            "django.contrib.auth",
            "django.contrib.contenttypes",
            "myapp",
        ],
    )  # Minimal Django settings required for our tests
    django.setup()  # configures Django
    TestRunner = get_runner(settings)  # Gets the test runner class
    test_runner = TestRunner()  # Creates an instance of the test runner
    failures = test_runner.run_tests(["tests"])  # Run tests and gather
                                                  failures
    sys.exit(bool(failures))  # Exits script with error code 1 if any failures
```

And using a settings module instead (from the following Django documentation). This is functionally the same as the preceding code except it breaks out the settings into a more typical settings file, in this case tests/test_settings.py

```python
#!/usr/bin/env python
import os
import sys

import django
from django.conf import settings
from django.test.utils import get_runner

if __name__ == "__main__":
    os.environ['DJANGO_SETTINGS_MODULE'] = 'tests.test_settings'
    django.setup()
    TestRunner = get_runner(settings)
    test_runner = TestRunner()
    failures = test_runner.run_tests(["tests"])
    sys.exit(bool(failures))
```

Why choose one over the other? Using a separate settings module will be more flexible if you have other needs for the settings. The in-script configuration style suffices for simpler apps, for example, those without models.

In Chapter 22 we'll examine a more *ergonomic* way of managing your tests and test configuration.

Testing application relationships

What happens though when your Django app is designed to be used with other apps, or used in conjunction with them? Testing only your app in isolation is not enough. In this case you'll need to create sample apps and include them in your test settings.

Let's say your app provides base models. For our example it's a very basic ecommerce module that lets people make a product out of any model they want, adding some basic fields like price, a SKU, and whether it's actively sold or not. The app also includes a queryset class with some helpful methods defined. Since our model class is abstract, the queryset class has to be associated with a concrete model in the user's app.

```
class ProductsQuerySet(models.QuerySet):
    def in_stock(self):
        return self.filter(is_in_stock=True)

class ProductBase(models.Model):
    sku = models.CharField()
    price = models.DecimalField()
    is_in_stock = models.BooleanField()

    class Meta:
        abstract = True
```

Now to test this, we need a concrete model (and it would be helpful to have tests actually using the base model anyhow). To do this we'll need another app that defines a concrete model inheriting from our abstract model, and that uses the provided queryset.

Such an app need only provide the bare minimum to be an app, specifically the models.py module:

```
test_app/
    migrations/ ...
    __init__.py
    models.py
```

And in your models file, define a model using your app's abstract base model:

```
from myapp.models import ProductBase, ProductQuerySet

class Pen(ProductBase):
    """Testing app model"""
    name = models.CharField()
    pen_type = models.CharField()
    objects = ProductQuerySet.as_manager()
```

With the models defined, make sure the test app is included in your test settings INSTALLED_APPS:

```
INSTALLED_APPS = [
    'myapp',
    'test_app',
]
```

Note that this applies to Django packages that are not installable apps as well if they require any level of integration testing.

Where to include tests

When you add tests to apps inside of your Django projects, you probably include test modules inside each app, either with a single file or a directory:

```
myapp/
    __init__.py
    models.py
        tests.py
```

This *will* work for standalone apps too, but generally should be avoided. Your tests in this case should live in a separate, top-level module outside of your app. If you're testing with additional modules, like test apps, then this ensures that there are no dependencies on non-installed modules within the code that ships with your app. It also keeps the installed package cleaner (although it's worth noting that this is not a unanimous opinion).

```
myapp/
    __init__.py
    models.py
test_app/
    __init__.py
    models.py
tests/
    __init__.py
    test_models.py
```

Testing without Django

The emphasis here is on Django apps, that is, Python modules that can be installed and included in a Django project to use models, template tags, management commands, among others. But in many cases the functionality provided by apps can be tested as plain old Python code.

This will be the case with anything in your app that requires setup, like models. However, this isn't true of every part of Django or every part of your app. And in fact if your app doesn't have any models, and you don't have any request-related functionality to test - especially at an integration test level - then you can forgo with setting up or using Django's test modules, sticking to the standard library's unittest, or any other testing framework you so choose.

You will only need to invoke a test runner through Django if you're loading the Django project, for example, anything involving models, settings, or a full request/response cycle. In most cases, testing features like forms, the logic in template tags and filters and others, is not dependent on any of the parts of Django that require project setup.

Why would you do this? It's extraordinarily doubtful that the performance gains from using unittest over django.test are going to be noticeable to say nothing of impactful. However, if these are the only tests that you need, then your testing environment will be simpler to set up and run.

Summary

In this chapter, you learned why it's important to have tests for your standalone app and how to begin testing a Django app when it's no longer part of a parent Django project. You also learned how to simplify test execution with a Python script that handles Django setup and how to test app features that are predicated on relationships defined by other apps outside of your own. Lastly, you learned where to include the tests for you standalone app, in a top-level tests directory, and that, for some types of apps that don't rely on the database or template engine, it may be sufficient to use Python's unittest library without the Django setup.

In the next chapter, you'll learn how to manage database migrations for your app without a Django project.

CHAPTER 4

Model migrations

Database migrations allow you to track changes in your database models and propagate them to the underlying database schema. If your standalone app includes *concrete models,* then you'll need to include migrations with your app. As with running tests, this is not fundamentally different in a standalone app than in an app in your own project; however, there are a few gotchas to watch out for.

In this chapter, you'll learn how to manage your app's database migrations outside of your Django project and a couple of practices that will make using these migrations safer and clearer.

Migrations outside of a project

When you create migrations for an app in your project, you simply run the management command to do this from project root:

```
./manage.py makemigrations app
```

With migrations then we run into the same problem as we did for running tests – we don't have a project from which to run the migrations command.

The runtests.py script used for running tests could be adapted to run the migration command; however, it'd be simpler to adopt an existing pattern: the manage.py script that ships with every Django project.

In your project root, create a manage.py file. The name itself is not important, but with this name its purpose will be obvious to you and anyone else. Just in the runtests. py example, you can configure Django directly from the file calling settings.configure or pointing to a separate settings module. The end result looks almost indistinguishable from the standard manage.py script.

```
import sys
import django
from django.conf import settings
```

© Ben Lopatin 2020

B. Lopatin, *Django Standalone Apps*, https://doi.org/10.1007/978-1-4842-5632-9_4

```
INSTALLED_APPS = [
    "django.contrib.auth",
    "django.contrib.admin",
    "django.contrib.contenttypes",
    "django.contrib.sites",
    "myapp",
]

settings.configure(
    DATABASES={
        "default": {
            "ENGINE": "django.db.backends.sqlite3",
        }
    },
    INSTALLED_APPS=INSTALLED_APPS,
    ROOT_URLCONF="tests.urls",
)

django.setup()

if __name__ == '__main__':
    from django.core.management import execute_from_command_line
    execute_from_command_line(sys.argv)
```

Testing migrations

Occasionally a developer pushes updates only to discover surprising failed builds, or, worse, a failed deployment, all because one or more migrations weren't added or included. This could be as simple as changing the value of a field, or adding an entirely new model and database table.

Alternatively, an update might work just fine, but the changes involved created a gap between the state of the current models and the state defined by the migrations. Changing an attribute on a model field is enough to do this, even if it doesn't entail any changes to the database schema. The problem in this scenario is that it puts end users in a situation where they may create the missing migration themselves, which when applied may conflict with subsequent migrations you add to the package.

Both scenarios can be avoided by double checking that there are no changes available to migrate. And better than double checking, this can be added to your automated test suite.

```
from django.test import TestCase
from django.core.management import call_command

class TestMigrations(TestCase):
    def test_no_missing_migrations(self):
        call_command("makemigrations", check=True, dry_run=True)
```

All the preceding test does is run the makemigrations command with two command line options, --check and --dry-run. The check flag makes the command exit with a failing, nonzero status if there are any changes detected, and the dry-run flag is just insurance that no other output is created. This test will then fail if you have missing migrations.

Additional migration guidelines

If you're not in the habit of descriptively naming your migrations, creating a standalone app is a good opportunity to pick up the habit. Django will try to provide a descriptive name if the migration is simple enough, but this isn't always possible, and instead you'll be left with timestamped migration. While it's true that you can read the source code, it'd be helpful to have an idea of the contents and purpose from the name. You specify the name for your files with the -n option:

```
./manage.py makemigrations myapp -n add_missing_choices
```

A good guideline for migration names is to treat them like even more concise Git commit message subjects: (i) what kind of change was made (e.g., adding, updating, removing) and (ii) the subject of the migration itself. This will help you later when you're adding new features and it will help contributors understand the progression of database changes.

Summary

In this chapter, you learned how to create database migrations for your standalone app by taking advantage of the same basic strategies used for testing outside of your project, how to add tests for missing migrations to your test suite, and why constructive migration naming is valuable. In the next chapter, we'll look at including HTML templates in your standalone app, including how to include them but just as important as what to include to optimize usefulness for your users.

CHAPTER 5

Templates

The mechanics of including HTML templates in your standalone app are no different than including templates in an app within a Django project. However, you do need to give careful consideration to naming and also to the content that you include in your templates. In this chapter, you'll learn how to name your templates for end users and how to optimize your template content for developer users.

Three basic strategies

If your app includes views that return rendered HTML responses, it'll be doing so by rendering HTML templates. Because of how Django loads templates, you have three options for handling initial template content:

1. Do not include the templates – after all, it's the user's site.

2. Include basic HTML templates.

3. Include detailed, even stylized, templates.

In most cases you should include *basic* HTML templates with your app that show both the rendered results during development and the structure of the template context included by your views.

What to include

The first option, shipping your standalone app without HTML templates that are referenced by your views should be considered a nonstarter. The primary benefit of excluding templates is that it makes it obvious where users of your app need to add their own templates. However, while the end users of your app are capable of providing their

© Ben Lopatin 2020
B. Lopatin, *Django Standalone Apps*, https://doi.org/10.1007/978-1-4842-5632-9_5

own templates, and you can document which ones should be included, it adds friction for using the app. It makes exploratory use more difficult and makes it less obvious what should be expected in the resulting template.

There is no bright line for differentiating between the second and third options, but beyond styling we can identify a more detailed template as one that introduces some combination of elements that are not strictly necessary to deliver the app's functionality. This brief template, which we might imagine included for a simple app view, introduces a couple of assumptions that are unnecessary.

```
{% extends "base.html" %}
{% block content %}
<h3>Here is a list of other fruits reported by the app</h3>
<ul>
{% for fruit in fruit_list %}
        <li class="fruit-{{fruit.category }}">{{ fruit }}</li>
{% endfor %}
</ul>
{% endblock content %}
```

We'd expect the page to render like Figure 5-1.

Figure 5-1. *Rendered web page*

While a good and popular convention, there's nothing that *requires* anyone to name a base template base.html, nor is there any requirement that if such a template exists, it should be the direct base template at this particular level. Likewise, there's no requirement that any project templates include a template block named content. It may make sense, and it may be the singularly most consistent thing you've ever seen used in Django projects, but it's still a convention by convenience. So while this template will create a richer initial experience for people with a base.html and content blocks, it'll fail for those who don't.

A far better strategy – in most cases – is to include basic templates that show a user the full range of template context with only minimal structure and styling. Here's the earlier example stripped down:

```
<h3>Here is a list of other fruits reported by the app.</h3>
<ul>
{% for fruit in fruit_list %}
        <li class="fruit-{{fruit.category }}">{{ fruit }}</li>
{% endfor %}
</ul>
```

The result in Figure 5-2 is not exciting, but the expectation is that users will be overriding our

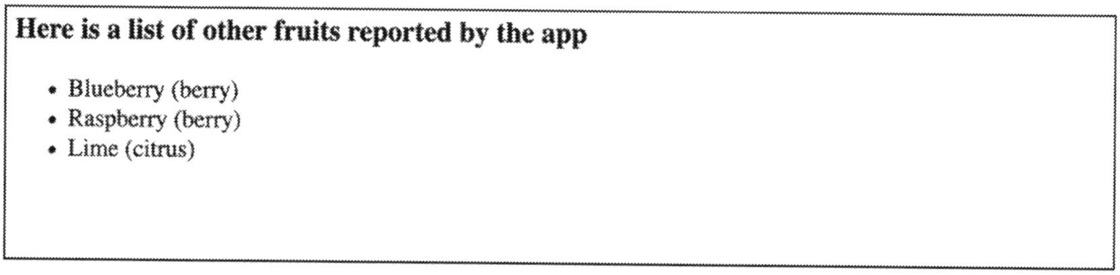

Here is a list of other fruits reported by the app

- Blueberry (berry)
- Raspberry (berry)
- Lime (citrus)

Figure 5-2. *Minimal structuring and styling*

templates eventually such that it's not valuable to make them look production ready in the shipped app.

There are cases where it is of use to provide significantly more detailed templates, namely, where the business goal of the app is to provide a stylized outcome, customized admin skins, for example.

It's a good idea to include translation strings in your templates but for simple example templates not necessary. Given the expectation that your developer users will be overriding these, they can include this or the language of their choice. See Chapter 13 for more on how to approach this problem.

Email and miscellaneous templates

The same that can be said about rendering HTML responses from views can be said about any other templated content, including emails. Email templates are a common feature in apps involving user registration, invitations, and any other kind of outbound notice.

The one addition with regard to email and notification templates is to include them in their own templates subfolder, for example, email/.

FLAT IS BETTER THAN NESTED: THE ZEN OF PYTHON

"Isn't using an extra directory unnecessary nesting?" Remember that practicality beats purity, and directories are "just" namespaces. The difference in namespace depth between myapp/email/welcome_body.html and myapp/email_welcome_body.html is zero; they're just split on a different character. The difference in viewing the folder system is that they're always obvious, both in the file system and, more importantly, in the calling source code.

Summary

In this chapter, you learned how best to include HTML templates in your standalone app and what to include in them. You learned that rather than including heavily styled templates that depend on specific base templates, it is better to include only the core structure of the template to demonstrate what is available in the template. In the next chapter, you'll learn how to include static assets like CSS and JavaScript to provide base styles and front-end functionality.

CHAPTER 6

Using static files

In your own Django projects, you likely have *static files*, static assets including style sheets, JavaScript, fonts, and images, all intended to be served directly to end users' browsers. These static files, or static assets, allow you to control the layout and styling of rendered HTML and introduce client-side (browser) interactivity.

While less common, some standalone apps may include their own *static files*, meant to be referenced either directly by name from an end user's project or through your own app's templates. Various types of standalone apps might use static files, typically including apps that provide custom admin functionality and apps bundling front-end framework components. In this chapter, we'll step through when it makes sense to include static assets in a standalone app and how to include them.

Static files in standalone apps

Historically there have been two primary reasons to include static files in a reusable app:

1. To add interface-based functionality provided by the app, for example, a core component of a greater whole.

2. To include static files for inclusion in a projects build process, for example, including a JavaScript framework so that when you run collectstatic, the required framework files are automatically available to the project.

The latter reason, including static files like a JS framework in the project, is largely obsolete. With the prevalence of front-end application code and build management systems like Gulp, Webpack, and Parcel, it's far more common for developers and teams to include and build these files from those build systems, in parallel to the Django static pipeline.

© Ben Lopatin 2020
B. Lopatin, *Django Standalone Apps*, https://doi.org/10.1007/978-1-4842-5632-9_6

If the purpose of the app is to include the Vue.js framework for inclusion in project templates, for example, it would be a better idea to eschew creating a Django app and configure a project JavaScript build system (like Webpack) to include the framework directly. Among other things, this enables fine-grained and portable control over JavaScript dependency versions.

That's not to say that there is no use case for creating a reusable app to provide this functionality. For smaller internal projects that don't warrant JavaScript build processes or very narrow use cases, this could still be beneficial.

Rather, the primary use case for including static files in a standalone Django app is to include interface-based functionality or styling. The mechanics of including static files are simple:

1. Add a static/ directory within your app directory.

2. Add your static files into your new static/ directory.

Note   We still have one more step to take to ensure these files are included in the final *package* for distribution, but this suffices to populate the project. Provided end users have app directory–based static file collection enabled (which is included by default), running collectstatic in a project with your app installed and in INSTALLED_APPS will copy these files to the project's STATIC_ROOT directory.

```
STATICFILES_FINDERS = [
        ...
        'django.contrib.staticfiles.finders.AppDirectoriesFinder',
]
```

It's important to note that when you run the collectstatic command to collect all of your project's static files, all of the files will be aggregated into the project's STATIC_ROOT directory including their path *relative* to your app's static directory.

What this means is that if you include static/style.css, it will be included as /static/style.css in the end project. This not only obscures the source of the file but also allows for naming conflicts.

As with templates, the solution is to include a named subdirectory to namespace the files:

```
myapp/
static/
                myapp/
                        style.css
        templates/
                myapp/
                list.html
```

Now your file will be available as /static/myapp/style.css. The final name of your assets may not be that critical if end users aggregate and minify these files, but you always want to avoid naming conflicts.

In the Django admin

If your Django app includes any kind of visual customization to the Django admin, from full-blown style replacement to minor JavaScript widgets, you can include the necessary files exactly as previously described. These files can be included in the same kind of directory-based namespace or using an admin/subdirectory. This is a good way of segmenting larger collections of files, although to avoid name conflicts, you should ensure files have app-specific names and/or use an additional layer of directory-based namespacing.

This layout will include myapp.css as /static/admin/myapp.css:

```
myapp/
        static/
                admin/
                        myapp.css
                myapp/
                        style.css
```

It is not necessary to use the admin/namespace for these files, however, especially if the only static files your app includes are admin specific. If on the other hand your app aims to *override* or supplant existing admin files, then you should namespace them such that the file paths are exactly the same as the files you want to override.

```
myapp/
        static/
                admin/
                        css/
                                login.css
```

Now provided myapp is included *after* django.contrib.admin in a project's INSTALLED_APPS, its login.css file will be used in place of Django's.

Lastly, if you include jQuery-based JavaScript for inclusion in the Django admin, make sure your plugins or functions are compatible with the version or versions that ship with the Django versions you aim to support. If you do this, and use the special namespacing employed by the Django admin – Django's admin uses the `django.jQuery` namespace for its included jQuery to avoid conflict with other introduced versions – you won't need to include jQuery yourself. On the other hand, if your bespoke functionality is dependent on a very specific version of jQuery for some reason, you'd want to include *that* version with your app. In this case, you can refer to using the "normal" jQuery namespace or your own, following Django's lead, to avoid any subsequent conflicts with any other introduced JavaScript.

Summary

In this chapter, you have learned how to include static assets in your standalone app, what kind of static assets make sense to include in your standalone app, and how to include JavaScript assets for Django admin–specific functionality. In the next chapter, we will further pursue the issue of namespacing, motivating the challenges and building up a set of strategies for creating sensible and coherent naming systems.

CHAPTER 7

Namespacing in your app

Namespaces are one honking great idea -- let's do more of those!

—The Zen of Python

In the previous several chapters, we walked through how to add several features to your app, including HTML templates and static files, which are organized and accessed by using app namespacing.

In this chapter, we'll learn how namespacing decisions pervade the rest of your standalone app and how to take advantage of namespacing to make integration and use of your app easier.

Namespaces at a glance

Namespaces are a way of organizing *named* objects – in Python and beyond – such that they have both a parent identifier and, more importantly, their names don't conflict. We've addressed namespaces a few times already, primarily in the context of template and static file directories, but their use extends well beyond configuring directories for collecting files.

With namespacing

- Two different modules can each define a function with the same name as the other, such that my_module.does_a_thing and your_module.does_a_thing don't conflict.

- Two different classes can each define a method with the same name as the other, such that MyClass.does_a_thing doesn't conflict with YourClass.does_a_thing.

© Ben Lopatin 2020
B. Lopatin, *Django Standalone Apps*, https://doi.org/10.1007/978-1-4842-5632-9_7

- Two different dictionaries can each contain the same key mapped to different values, such that my_dict["key"] = 4 while your_dict["key"] = 1.

The use of varied namespaces is easy to take for granted in your own project, but when introducing code into varied Django projects, you should take the time to ensure it's sensibly namespaced.

App itself

Our entrypoint to namespacing a standalone Django app is the app itself, more specifically, its module name and how it's named in its AppConfig. This is the easiest but also most important step. In order to avoid name collisions in Django project codebases, and, more importantly, to make distinctions obvious, the app name should be descriptive and not obviously overlap known existing app names, either those that ship with Django or are published for shared use.

If, for example, you built a standalone app for interfacing with the Stripe billing service, you might be tempted to name it stripe. But if you did this, you'd run into conflicts with the authoritative Stripe Python SDK. Instead, you might decide to name it something related to Django, like django_stripe or djstripe, except now the latter at least conflicts with an existing published standalone app! If your app is a substitute for the functionality of djstripe, then they're unlikely to be used in the same project and thus collide; however, unless your app is a fork of djstripe, it's likely to cause confusion for developers working with the app. In this case choose a different name.

When the descriptive name for an app is unavailable or ill-advised because of a conflict, choosing an adapted name with extra context, like stripe_billing, or using a synonym or allusion, works too, like zebra. The zebra app is a now unmaintained app for integrating Stripe payments in Django projects, so named because zebras have stripes.

URLs

There are multiple ways of adding namespaces to URLs to make identifying them in a project obvious and to avoid naming conflicts. In the event of a naming conflict, the first matching *named URL* will be used. This can be confusing especially if no exception is raised.

It's entirely possible to use the base URL name itself to establish the namespace. There's little *fundamental* difference between myapp_list and myapp:list. The latter is clearer about where the namespace "breaks," but both ensure that a list-related view is unique to the myapp name.

Settings

If your standalone app allows configuration via django.conf.settings, then these will also need to be consistently namespaced. What may work locally in your own Django project is not guaranteed to work across every other project.

For example, for an app called organizations that manages accounts with multiple users, you might have several settings that regulate the user model to use, the number of members allowed per group, and whether admin users can invite new members:

```
GROUP_USER_MODEL = AUTH_USER_MODEL
GROUPS_LIMIT = 8
ADMINS_CAN_INVITE = True
```

While confusing enough in the original Django project, the scope of impact is quite limited. Transferring this motley set of names across projects in a reusable app scales out the problem however. So instead, ensure that each setting *as named in the project settings* has a consistent preface, for example:

```
ORGANIZATIONS_USER_MODEL = AUTH_USER_MODEL
ORGANIZATIONS_USER_LIMIT = 8
ORGANIZATIONS_ADMINS_CAN_INVITE = True
```

For more on structuring settings and handling defaults within apps, see Chapter 7.

Management commands

Django's management commands function as command line–based interfaces to Django projects. A good way to think about them is *views* but for terminal processing instead of HTTP requests. There are many reasons for a standalone app to include management commands: syncing data, importing and exporting data, or providing a way to create default data.

For a quick review, management command names come from the module (file) name. A module within management/commands in an app that defines a subclass of BaseCommand simply named Command will be treated as a named management command by Django.

```
myapp/
        __init__.py
        management/
                __init__.py
                commands/
                        __init__.py
                        migrate_user_data.py
```

Unlike URL names, however, management command names are global. If you want to include a management command that will *migrate* user data across systems, using the name migrate would conflict with the Django ORM's migrate command, overriding the base migrate command causing no small amount of heartburn.

Two solutions present themselves for both avoiding name conflicts and making clear the purpose of the command:

1. Prefacing the command name (module name) with an application identifier

2. Making each command name as descriptive and unique as possible

Using the application name as a namespace for management commands is not a common practice, but this doesn't mean it's not a good one. This is a good strategy if your app has several management commands or if your app has a simple name. Both django-jet and dj-stripe follow this practice, prefacing management commands with jet_ and dj_stripe, respectively. In the case of dj-stripe, this means that a command to sync_models is clearly defined as being related to dj-stripe, instead of being a globally ambiguous command.

In the case of management commands, making the command names explicit even without a name prefix is often sufficient. This can involve including the app name elsewhere or referencing something unique to the app, like a class of data or service. django-cachalot provides the invalidate_cachalot management command, which is both an obviously app-specific name and also clear in what it does. django-reversions provides createinitialrevisions and deleterevisions.

Absent a URL-like namespacing scheme for management commands, which strategy you choose will be context dependent.

Template tags

There's no limit on how many modules you put in the templatetags package. Just keep in mind that a {% load %} statement will load tags/filters for the given Python module name, not the name of the app.

—Django docs

Template tags – and filters – add both logical and formatting functionality to templates at render time. Adding new template tags is as simple as including a templatetags module in your app and then one or more tag libraries as submodules.

```
myapp/
        templatetags/
                __init__.py
                myapp_tags.py
```

Template tags and filters present two namespacing challenges:

1. The tag library names are global, that is, not namespaces with regard to the app.

2. Individual tags and filters are similarly loaded into a single namesapce, though only in the context of a template that loads the library.

The implication is that you should aim to use name prefixing to keep your template tag modules uniquely named and name individual tags and filters such that they're implicitly app namespaced, at least where they provide some kind of app-specific functionality. If the tags or filters are intended to be used or useful beyond the context of data in your app, then it may make sense to name them more generally.

Models and database tables

App models and their respective database table names have default namespaces thanks to the application name itself. A project could have fifteen different apps each with its own model class named User and this would not pose any special conflict, so long as they're imported with aliases where they might come into conflict.

```
from app1.models import User as UserApp1
from app2.models import User as UserApp2
from app3.models import User as UserApp3
```

Nonetheless, import conflicts are not the only issues we seek to avoid with naming but also descriptiveness. Where a model both serves in a very app-specific way (i.e., it would be difficult to construe how it could be used outside of the app) and it is expected to be used with other models outside of the app, then *app-specific* naming should be used.

```
class MyAppUser(models.User):
        """A user model specific to the myapp app"""
```

Database table naming is largely an afterthought in developing Django projects since the ORM generates default table names. While there's something to be said about creating descriptive and human friendly table names, the primary concern for a reusable app is simply that the app preface in the table name can be expected to be unique.

Let's say you have an app that provides a kind of user-facing logging, and you name the app logs; it's not a very good name for a standalone app, but let's take it as a given. The database table names will be prefaced with logs_, for example, for a model named LogEntry, the table name would be logs_logentry.

If you're writing any SQL outside of the Django application, the table name lacks the context that the model class does in the scope of the source code. So in this example, if you absolutely had to maintain the app name logs, then it would be wise to specify db_table values in your model Meta classes:

```
class LogEntry(models.Model):
    ...

    class Meta:
            db_table = "activitylogs_logentry"
```

Now, anyone writing SQL queries or inspecting the database will have a much clearer understanding of what the table represents and what kind of data it contains.

CHAPTER 8

Creating a basic package

The last item left in taking a Django app and making it standalone is turning it into an installable package. This itself is a rich topic which we'll revisit in more depth in Chapter 18, but for now our goal is to meet the minimum requirements to make a simple Django app installable from outside the Django project.

An example blog app

The simple blog app has been used for countless tutorials and examples, and where it would otherwise be stale, here it lets us focus on the new features as a working *standalone* app.

We'll go into greater detail about setting up a package in Section 4, but this will be enough to create a package that is testable, deployable, and publishable. Our blog app is very simple, including only one model, Post, two views post_list and post_detail and their respective URLs, a single template filter for rendering reading times, basic templates for the two views, and a single CSS file for initial blog styles.

```
blog
├── __init__.py
├── admin.py
├── apps.py
├── migrations
│   ├── 0001_initial.py
│   ├── __init__.py
├── models.py
├── static
│   └── blog
│       └── blog.css
│
```

© Ben Lopatin 2020

B. Lopatin, *Django Standalone Apps*, https://doi.org/10.1007/978-1-4842-5632-9_8

```
├── templates
│   └── blog
│       ├── post_detail.html
│       └── post_list.html
├── templatetags
│   ├── __init__.py
│   └── blog_tags.py
├── urls.py
└── views.py
```

We'll include the blog app directory in the root blog_app directory, in addition to our files for running tests and creating migrations.

```
blog_app
├── blog
├── manage.py
├── runtests.py
├── setup.py
|-- tests
```

The one thing we've included here is the setup.py file.

A basic setup.py file

In order to package this, we need a way of defining the package: what is it called, what version is it, and where is the code. If you're familiar with Ruby Gemspec or Node package.json files, the setup.py file serves a similar purpose. And it's just Python. Let's look at the file.

```
from setuptools import setup, find_packages

setup(
    name="blog",
    version="0.1.0",
```

```
    author="Ben Lopatin",
    author_email="ben@benlopatin.com",
    url="http://www.django-standalone-apps.com",

    packages=find_packages(exclude=["tests"]),
)
```

This is about as basic and stripped down as we can get. This isn't enough to release our package, but it should be enough to build it so we can install it locally as a standalone Python package.

The ordering of the arguments to the setup function is not meaningful since they are keyword arguments, and they are grouped and spaced here only for convenience of explanation:

1. The first argument is the package name. If this is omitted, you can still create a build directory for your package, but any build artifacts, from wheel files to zipped source code, will be named UNTITLED obviating publishing and installing elsewhere.

2. The second argument specifies the *version number*. This is critical for replacing older versions when bug fixes or new features are released.

3. The author name, which would be you.

4. Author email, which is your email address.

5. Project URL, which indicates where someone can find more information about the project (e.g. documentation site, source repository).

6. The final line specifies *where the package is to be found*. This is the critical argument, and here by relying on the find_packages function, we can avoid having to specify individual path names.

With this file we can run python setup.py check and see that we are not missing anything and then run python setup.py build to generate a copy of the package as it will appear in distributed form in the build/ directory.

Adding templates and static files

If you build the project using the python setup.py build command and list the files in your newly created (or updated) build/ directory, you'll find that your template and static asset files are missing:

```
build/
        lib/
                blog/
                        __init__.py
                        admin.py
                        apps.py
                        migrations/
                                0001_initial.py
                                __init__.py
                        models.py
                        templatetags/
                                __init__.py
                                blog_tags.py
                        urls.py
                        views.py
```

This is because setuptools only look for Python files to include in your package (and a few *specific* non-Python files as well). In order to include these, we'll need to include a manifest file, that is, MANIFEST.in.

The MANIFEST.in file allows you to specify files that should be included in your package using a very simple named or wildcard format. In our case, we don't want to have to necessarily specify every single template and static asset individually, so we'll want to make use of wildcards. For examples sake, and because we only have the one CSS file, we'll use both.

```
include blog/static/blog/blog.css
recursive-include blog/templates *.html
```

Both lines specify files by location with regard to the directory root, that is, the MANIFEST.in parent directory. The first line includes a single file by path name, while the second will include all HTML files located in the blog/templates directory, including subdirectories. Files matching these lines will be copied into the build product along with the Python files.

Now if you build your app using python setup.py build, you will find your static and templates directories including all of your CSS, JavaScript, and HTML templates:

```
build/
    lib/
        blog/
                __init__.py
                admin.py
                apps.py
                migrations/
                        0001_initial.py
                        __init__.py
                models.py
                static/
                        blog/
                                blog.css
                templates/
                        blog/
                                post_detail.html
                                post_list.html
                templatetags/
                        __init__.py
                        blog_tags.py
                urls.py
                views.py
```

Installing and using

There are two ways to install a usable, local copy of your app now. You can run python setup.py install which will predictably install a copy of your app into the site-packages directory relevant to your current Python path (e.g., system Python site-packages or a virtualenv site-packages). Or you can run python setup.py develop. This will instead install a link from site-packages to your project root in the form of a file named blog.egg-info which contains the path to your package.

The benefit of using the develop command is that since your package directory is *effectively* symlinked into your site-packages, every change to your package is immediately available anywhere you are using that package. Thus it makes it easier to develop a package, here your standalone app, in parallel with another project without having to reinstall with every change.

The downside is that you may end up developing the other project against an untagged version of your standalone app (i.e., a specific release). The risk then is that your other package doesn't accurately capture the features or the published API of your standalone app. You may also run into conflicts if you try to install your app in your Python environment using python setup.py develop and then subsequently install using pip. As such this should be used for exploratory work and not as a full-time strategy for installing your standalone apps.

In Chapter 18 we'll delve into some improved strategies for building a package that make maintenance easier and publishing to share simpler.

Summary

In this chapter, you learned about the basic structure and requirements of creating an installable Python package for your standalone app. This provides a minimal first step to working with your standalone app outside the context of your Django project and gives you a foundation to publish on a package index. In the next chapter, we'll begin looking at how to assess and extract a standalone app from part of your existing Django project.

PART II

Scoping and Extracting a Reusable App

CHAPTER 9

Scoping and drawing boundaries

In the first chapter, we discussed in brief what it means to *scope* a Django standalone app, including your goals in creating a standalone app, the considerations of third-party dependencies, and the *job* the app is expected to perform.

In this chapter, we'll revisit these same considerations in more depth and specifically with respect to looking at a possible Django standalone app in the context of an existing codebase.

Scoping and the nature of the problem

Defining the scope of a software project is one of the first challenges in a project, and one of the most important. The scope defines what it will do and where the boundaries are and influences not just the size of a project in lines of code but also how complicated it is, how many features it can support, and how challenging it is to test and maintain the software.

The app as written in your own project may have an explicit scope, but it's easy for the boundaries to become blurred when it's an integrated part of your project source code. This may be because of feature creep or because of some immediate convenience – it was simpler or more expedient to include some new small feature within the app even though the purpose of that feature is orthogonal to the app's core job, or is overly specific to your particular project.

The scope of the app will influence what dependencies are required as well. As the "dependency surface area" increases, so does the brittleness of the app with regard to maintenance and version support. If your standalone app depends on Django, then it's simply tied to Django versions. If however it requires Django, and one or more

© Ben Lopatin 2020
B. Lopatin, *Django Standalone Apps*, https://doi.org/10.1007/978-1-4842-5632-9_9

additional standalone apps, then it's most likely limited by the degree to which all of the dependencies overlap in their support of Django and Python versions. Reducing the scope of your standalone app from what you might have included in your own project has the expected effect of making it far simpler to maintain.

The job of a standalone app

What would you say you do here?

If you're looking for a heuristic for scoping and defining the boundaries of the app, you can do worse than to simply write a brief job description. As an employee you may have an ill-fitting job title and a multitude of varied responsibilities, but if you strip it down, then more than likely you can define a purpose for your job beyond the things you do. As a software developer, your job is to translate business needs into working software. As a CEO your job is to lead the company to growth and profitability (in most places, at least). There may be more job responsibilities, and these may be important, but nearly every job has a singular purpose. Likewise, your standalone app should have a guiding purpose that can be briefly and concisely described.

Put yourself in the shoes of a marketer (no, really). How would you describe your app? What problem does it solve? How does it solve that problem? How does it solve this problem for many other applications?

The answers to these questions *will* be helpful in marketing an open source package, but that's not why we're asking them.

Here are several popular standalone Django apps and, in my own words, their brief job description:

- The job of **Wagtail** is to make it easier to model and serve user-editable content in a user friendly way.

- The job of **Django REST Framework** is to provide a Django-like experience for creating RESTful APIs and connecting existing Django apps to the API.

- The job of **django-taggit** is to make it easy to add tags, in the taxonomical sense, to any kind of object in a Django project

- The job of **Easy Thumbnails** is to create resized images for a single uploaded image.

These apps vary in their size and the scope of features they provide, but in each case all of those features can be traced back to a singularly stated purpose.

The dimensions for creation and extraction

There are a number of dimensions by which you can look at a standalone app; here I want to focus on the axis that I'll call vertical and horizontal segmentation, or in other words, business feature vs. technical foundation. In the following figure, we see that a feature (yellow bar) is a vertical slice through the horizontal components of any app or project (Figure 9-1).

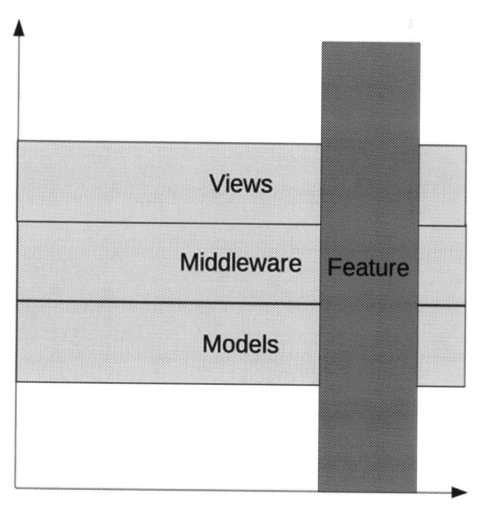

Figure 9-1. *Vertical and horizontal segmentation*

Do not be persuaded that this allows for some kind of scientific taxonomy; rather, it's a handy way of assessing how modules are broken up and organized and, in the context of standalone Django apps, how to define the job they do.

Horizontally segmented modules – apps or otherwise – provide some kind of common "infrastructure" that can be used across projects that supports the development of features. This is code that delivers something only a developer will experience (by and large).

Examples include

- django-model-utils

- django-extensions

- django-crisyforms

These primarily solve problems that development teams face, like making it easier to render complex forms and providing common base classes to avoid repeated boilerplate code.

Horizontally organized code within a project looks like this, emphasizing organization by *what the code does first* and what business domain it solves for second:

```
app/
        forms/
        models/
                ...
                image_models.py
                user_models.py
                subscription_models.py
        views/
```

This will look familiar since this is the convention for organizing code *within* a Django app, but it's also the convention for organizing project code in other frameworks.

Vertically segmented modules, on the other hand, are organized first around a business need, that is to say, usually something that a user will experience.

Examples include

- django.contrib.auth

- Haystack

- django-suit

It should be obvious that this isn't an "either/or" distinction of course. But Django's app-centric architecture encourages vertical or feature-based organization. A Django app includes everything from models to URL routes to forms and views. This is necessarily how standalone apps ship, but this is also the default pattern for apps within a Django project.

If the functionality you're targeting looks like something that's feature agnostic, it probably warrants inclusion in an app separate from features.

Sizing the scope of an app

A standalone Django app should be big enough to do its job, and no bigger. But how big is that? What are the consequences of mis-sizing the scope a standalone app? And how can you solve for an app that looks too small or unwieldy large?

First, an app should be no bigger than its job. But it should also be big enough. If it is too big, it's either doing too much, or it's another framework in and of itself. Too small and it may not warrant creating a standalone app, or even an installable package.

When an app is too big

What does it mean for an app to be too big? There are some rather large standalone apps that aren't necessarily too big. The answer is as clear as mud: *it depends*. The first thing that makes an app too big is including extraneous features that either aren't critical to the app or would be sufficiently useful in their *own app*. A tractable example of this would be an app that includes its own utility base classes, like the kind you'd find in django-model-utils. These extra features can become distractions when maintaining the app and adding features down the road. They increase the amount of code that needs to be tested, as well. Don't jettison them if they're necessary, but make sure they're necessary.

A couple of solutions stand out for apps that are too large:

- Break it up into separate packages.

- Organize into sub-apps.

Breaking into separate packages is a good idea if at least one of the potential packages is sufficiently useful on its own. The benefit of separate packages in such a case is of a wider net for more use cases. However, each additional package, whether a standalone app or not, increases the cost of maintenance and may make it more challenging to ensure that the two components continue to work well together.

If they're mutually interdependent, then there's no benefit in creating separate packages, and using sub-apps or mini apps in a single package is a superior choice.

Organizing a standalone app into sub-apps requires then that each app be added individually to a target project's INSTALLED_APPS like so:

```
INSTALLED_APPS = [
    ...
    "cms",
    "cms.pages",
    "cms.photos",
    ...
]
```

This strategy consists of a primary, top-level app with subsidiary and constituent feature apps included as their own installable apps. While clunkier than adding only the one "core" app, this may allow you to better structure the components logically and to allow developer users to exclude functionality that they don't need. This doesn't reduce the footprint of your app's source code, but it does reduce the scope that anyone using the app must consider.

When an app is too small

The problems of making an app that is too small are different and arguably less significant than those of an app that is too large. The main issue is that it risks leading to a preponderance of tiny dependencies that all need to be included and maintained. The benefit of using standalone packages decreases when their number transcends what you can easily remember. And we'd like to minimize the dependencies our app introduces into other people's projects.

If you are looking at creating multiple small apps, first consider whether they really make sense on their own, or if they have sufficient commonality, in either functionality or business domain to bundle together. If you find yourself using these features together in more than one project, that is likely the case.

Creating a tiny standalone app shouldn't be treated as forbidden though. And there's an obvious tension between the two ends of the spectrum.

Summary

In this chapter, you learned how to approach scoping your app, by defining the job that the app is to accomplish, by assessing the possible feature and component dimensions of the app, and additionally identifying how the size of the scope can be assessed and adjusted. In the next chapter, we'll learn how to begin the process of refactoring and extracting your app from an existing Django project.

CHAPTER 10

Separating your app

While some packages start their lives fully born as standalone installable libraries, it's more typical to begin in one form or another as functionality in an existing project. This may be spread throughout or in its own app within the project.

The goal in this chapter is to extract functionality from one or more apps, either removing a monolith or consolidating functionality from across multiple apps and putting this into a distinct and project-agnostic app in your project. That means not only its own individual app but one that "knows" nothing about nor depends on the specifics of your original Django project.

Getting started

For example, this might mean extracting and removing specific subscription plan information out from a software-as-a-service (SaaS) project. It means using only settings that are core to Django or specific to the app. And it often means dropping the assumption of specific backend services such as an email provider or cloud file storage provider where this assumption is not necessary to the core functionality of the app.

The key to all of this is understanding where your app(s) *currently fit* in your project's *hierarchy of dependence* and where they *ought to* fit in that hierarchy. The hierarchy of dependence describes how various modules are related to each other in a Django project (it can be used with any software project, even an individual Python package, too) and which depend on each other. It includes your soon-to-be-standalone app, project-specific Django apps, other third-party standalone Django apps, Django itself, third-party Python packages that are Django-agnostic, and even the Python standard library.

Diagram of architecture here. We want to show that you're pull foundational apps or perhaps from above, what this is depending on.

Thus our goal is to move the app *up* the hierarchy of dependence, if necessary, so that it is used in outside Django projects.

B. Lopatin, *Django Standalone Apps*, https://doi.org/10.1007/978-1-4842-5632-9_10

Refactor first

Anytime you're coming back to or even starting to work on code, there is going to be a temptation to rewrite or edit the source code, or what's popularly referred to as refactoring. In its original meaning however, refactoring means only modifying the code without affecting how it works, or in Martin Fowler's words (emphasis added):

> *Refactoring is the process of changing a software system in such a way that it does not alter the external behavior of the code yet **improves its internal structure**.*

> —Refactoring, 1st Ed., Martin Fowler

The term's colloquial meaning is much looser, and it's often used to describe any kind of editing to source code. Here however we focus on the stricter definition of refactoring. This includes things from reformatting the source code to renaming variables, up to breaking apart or moving functions, methods, classes, and even modules. It does not involve adding new functions or replacing algorithms. Those may be good or even necessary steps, but they are not refactoring.

Despite using the word *temptation* with regard to refactoring, refactoring is a good thing. It tends to make code easier to understand and easier to reuse as well. These are desirable benefits in extracting a standalone app. However, in some cases, it can become a distraction if it obscures other changes undertaken in the code, so when there is an estimated level of refactoring ahead, it makes sense to tackle that first. This gets it out of the way and makes the code easier to work with for the more significant efforts.

Code formatting – from standardized indentation to the organization of package imports – is a great starting point. The *diffs* in your code can be helpful to track as you progress, and these are less useful if they're filled with spurious changes. If you decide to use an autoformatter like black and you haven't before, its first run may result in a large diff. Isolate this first as a commit and move on, so you know what changes you made and which were just cleaning up whitespace.

Next you'll likely want to rename some variables or functions, especially if they're named in such a way that's overly reflective of the larger Django project. The second reason for undertaking this refactoring as the first step is that changes to function and class names, function signatures, or class initialization signatures will likely cascade into your existing Django project. There's a benefit to front loading as much of this work as possible, so that subsequent updates can focus as narrowly as possible on the app itself.

Model renaming and migrations

Renaming your models and/or database tables is a refactoring exercise, but it comes with some Django-specific caveats. This is because changes to the class and even module name of Django models affects the migration state, as well as the default database table name when the table name is not explicitly specified. And carelessly changing table names in this way can be destructive.

The first step is to ensure your app models use a common and sensible database table namespace. Your existing app name may not be appropriate for a standalone app, and it's possible too that your models started life in another app within your project. As a result the table names might be inconsistent and they might be insignificantly descriptive.

So for each model in your app, ensure that it has its current table name explicitly named in the model's Meta class:

```
class LogCategory(models.Model):
    class Meta:
        db_table = "tracking_logcategory"

class Entry(models.Model):
    class Meta:
        db_table = "someapp_entry"
```

At this point you should create a migration file that captures this state change, though at this time it will have no effects on the database (since the name is not actually changing):

```
class Migration(migrations.Migration):

    dependencies = [
        ('myapp', '0001_initial'),
    ]

    operations = [
        migrations.AlterModelTable(
            name='entry',
            table='someapp_entry',
        ),
    ]
```

The second step is to rename these tables, as necessary, using the Meta.db_ table attribute:

```
class LogCategory(models.Model):
        class Meta:
                db_table = "tracking_logcategory"

class Entry(models.Model):
        class Meta:
                db_table = "tracking_entry"
```

Again, create an individual migration file for this change. The resulting migration when run will alter the underlying database table names but otherwise not affect the structure of your database.

```
class Migration(migrations.Migration):

    dependencies = [
        ('myapp', '0001_initial'),
    ]

    operations = [
        migrations.AlterModelTable(
            name='entry',
            table='tracking_entry',
        ),
    ]
```

At this point you are free to rename the model classes within your app without affecting the database.

> One point: If you have many-to-many fields defined on any of your app's models, you should ensure you have an explicitly defined through model with a table name defined in the preceding example. You will need to start with the existing table name as well.

A further wrinkle you may run into if you're moving model classes between apps –for example, extracting a project-specific model or consolidating a few models – is that Django migrations when models change apps are *destructive*. If we want to move a model out of an app, here's the resultant migration:

```
class Migration(migrations.Migration):

    dependencies = [
        ('myappp', '0001_initial'),
    ]

    operations = [
        migrations.DeleteModel(
            name='Entry',
        ),
    ]
```

That migration operation right there is a deletion and if run would result in dropping the underlying database table. There are, of course, various ways around this. You could fake the migration, running ./manage.py migrate myapp 0001 --fake, for example, to advance the migration state without affecting the database. This subsequently needs to be executed for the target or recipient app and suffice to say is a bit cumbersome in local development. It's downright nasty to try orchestrating in production deployments.

You could also subclass the migration operation class, to make its database_forwards method not do anything, thus effecting no change in the database:

```
class DeleteNothing(migrations.DeleteModel):
    def database_forwards(self, *args, **kwargs):
        """Do nothing"""
        pass
```

This is arguably superior to faking migrations, but similarly cumbersome, potentially confusing, and thankfully unnecessary. This is a use case for the migrations. SeparateDatabaseAndState operation class.

A database migration like our DeleteModel has two effects: one on the database, which we're trying to prevent from happening, and one on the cumulative state of the app's models. The latter we do need. The migrations.SeparateDatabaseAndState class allows you to separate out the two, so that the *state affecting* migrations can be run. The result is an updated migration state that "knows" what the table name is and that won't effect any changes on the underlying database.

Implementing this is simple; we insert the class initializing call in the top-level Migration.operations and then move the deleting operation into the state_operations keyword argument to SeparateDatabaseAndState. The previous migration then becomes this:

```
class Migration(migrations.Migration):

    dependencies = [
        ('myappp', '0001_initial'),
    ]

    operations = [
                migrations.SeparateDatabaseAndState(
                        state_operations=[
                        migrations.DeleteModel(
                            name='Entry',
                        ),
                        ]
                )
    ]
```

When run, this will advance the state of the myapp migration history so that the Entry model is no longer a part of the app, but it will not make any changes to the database.

Allowing customization

Likely your app makes some assumptions that are based on *your use of it*. These could include specific backing services or even workflows that are close to what you'd need in another project but still sufficiently over-specific to be useful as shared functionality. There are a few ways of accounting for this, and while not **necessary** to do now, it is advantageous to make these changes while they're still in your working project.

Backend classes

You've probably used standalone apps that provide options for customized functionality, including

- django-anymail (email)

- django-allauth (authentication)

- Haystack (search)

Each of these solves a specific business problem that has several solutions. In the case of the aforementioned apps, this is accomplished by allowing the developer user to pick a specific backend or provider. As with database support in the Django ORM, each defined backend or provider handles the specifics required for that integration, but exposes a common interface to the developer user for a seamless experience.

The crux of using this option is that every backend or provider class inherits from a base class or otherwise matches a base interface. If your app is supposed to manage a workflow, but currently has a very project-specific workflow, this workflow can be moved into a separate module in your project and referenced by import in the app.

In the project settings, you might require a dotted path to the class or module:

```
MYAPP_WORKFLOW = "core.workflows.CustomerWorkflow"
```

And then in your app, where you have a requirement to kick off this workflow, you can simply import the correct class or module by path:

```
from django.conf import settings
from django.utils.module_loading import import_string

def get_myapp_workflow():
        """Returns the class by dotted path from settings"""
        import_string(backend or MYAPP_WORKFLOW)

def run_workflow():
        """Calls the user/project defined class"""
        workflow_class = get_myapp_workflow()
        customer_workflow = workflow_class().start()
        ...
```

Signals

Django's signals provide for a way of dispatching named events and handling them with synchronous callback functions. The prototypical examples include Django's built-in signals emitted at lifecycle milestones in ORM objects, including pre_save, post_save, pre_delete, and post_delete.

Signals allow you to respond to these events, from specific classes, and modify the objects in question or trigger some other workflow as a result of the specific action or parameters. When overly used, signals can be confusing, obfuscating the flow of the program, making it harder to debug, to test, to manage performance, and on the whole to maintain. *That being said,* they do solve the problem of how to change how some object is treated or how some function should work when you know access to the originating code is unavailable. For example, it would be trivial to add some statements to the save method of a model class in your own project; this becomes infeasible when working with a standalone app.

```
class Entry(models.Model):
        def save(self, **kwargs):
                some_webhook(self)
                return super().save(**kwargs)
```

Especially if the custom functionality looks like a one off, or is a way of tying changes in one model to another such that it follows a fairly standard pattern marked out by Django itself, signals can help you unravel project-specific logic from your app and keeping it in your project:

```
from django.db.models.signals import pre_save
from django.dispatch import receiver
from myapp.models import Entry

@receiver(pre_save, sender=MyModel)
def webhook_sender(sender, **kwargs):
        some_webhook(kwargs["instance"])
```

And if you're looking for somewhere to be liberal with debug logging, signal handlers are a good place to start.

Finalization and removing from the project

As a last step before removing the code, take this opportunity to clean up and squash the app migrations so that when you remove the code from the project, it starts life without any references to your project. And nobody wants to run spurious migrations.

Once the code has been extracted, you can move it out of the project. There's no need to race off and publish to the Python Package Index (PyPI) just yet.

From here you can include the code in your project as a submodule, using Git, or set up the basics of an installable package and include the requirement from a remote source repository. This allows you to start using a single codebase in multiple projects.

Summary

In this chapter, we reviewed some strategies from *removing* your app from your project, including how to preserve your existing database structures and how to enable project-level customization when the app code is no longer part of the project.

In the next chapter, we'll look at some strategies for adding your app back into your project.

CHAPTER 11

Adding your app back in

Extracting your app from your project entails several steps:

1. Refactoring the app

2. Moving it to a top-level namespace (if necessary)

3. Removing it from the project

Step three leaves you with a conundrum if you want to continue using the app in your original project(s). Unless you have no need for your new standalone app or, as may be the case in some instances, you need to keep an original, un-refactored source in your project, you'll need to include the new standalone app in the project or projects that spawned it.

Verifying locally

The first step is to verify integration using your project from a locally installed source outside of your project. For this you can rely on installing within your project's Python environment using python setup.py develop as described in Chapter 8. Note that if your project is only available via a virtual machine (e.g., using Vagrant) or a container (e.g., Docker), it would be expeditious to skip to the next step with regard to deployment.

Our presumption at this point is that you have removed the app from your project, either from the project root or the project repository altogether, such that it's not in the project path. At the very least, this means if you try to run your project without installing the app in some explicit way, you can expect to run into an ImportError or two.

However, simply installing from the app's own root outside of the project root means that you can verify that the project still runs as expected with the code removed from the project itself.

© Ben Lopatin 2020
B. Lopatin, *Django Standalone Apps*, https://doi.org/10.1007/978-1-4842-5632-9_11

Source control–based packages

Installing and using your app from a locally installed package works fine for testing and developing new features, but it won't work when it's time to deploy your project. For this we'll need the app available remotely, and a simple way to start is by providing the package via source control. As a starting point, or for private reusable apps without a private package index, this is an easy starting point.

The Python package installer, pip, allows you to install packages a number of ways. You can of course provide nothing more than the package name, and pip will look for the named package on the Python Package Index. However, pip can also install packages from remote source control links, that is, Git repositories.

The full details are documented on the pip website itself, but in short it works by providing (i) the version control protocol, (ii) the path to the repository, and (iii) the target package name. In the following example, the package myapp is installed from a Git repo with the full path to the Git repository:

```
pip install git://githost.org/myapp.git@v1.0#egg=myapp
```

This example also installs a specific version by using a Git tag. The fragment @v1.0 is comprised of two parts: the @ which indicates that what follows is a named *head* in the repository, that is, a branch name, tag name, or commit SHA, and the rest which is that name itself. Then the end of the line, egg=myapp, is what specifies the target package name.

This can be added to a requirements.txt file just like a package name.

If you were installing this from your GitHub repository, the same line would look like this, presuming your username is me:

```
pip install git://github.com/me/myapp.git@v1.0#egg=myapp
```

The source control version specification using a tag or commit is technically optional, but for the purposes of actually installing packages using this strategy, you should always use a commit version either by tag name or commit SHA. Branch names may be tempting but are moving targets and will not allow you to effectively declare a version.

The advantages of using and installing your package from Git rather than from the Python Package Index (PyPI) are mostly related to control and the overhead of publishing a package. You don't need to register the name on PyPI, you don't need to build anything, and you don't need to seriously worry about the changelog or if your package metadata is correct. These are not weighty concerns, but if you just want to start reusing your app yourself, you can skip those preliminaries at first.

The limitations include not just decreased visibility, which is provided by being on PyPI and being installable via a short pip install myapp, but also less reusability. The visibility affects this, but more than anything the lack of sequentially available versions is the obstacle. Using Git tags and commit SHAs lets you pin specific versions, which is an excellent strategy for individual projects, but an untenable one for other packages, as you lose the ability to select versions based on ranges (e.g., django>=3.0). When packages pin the versions of their requirements, they will force that version in the environment, even when other packages may require the same package.

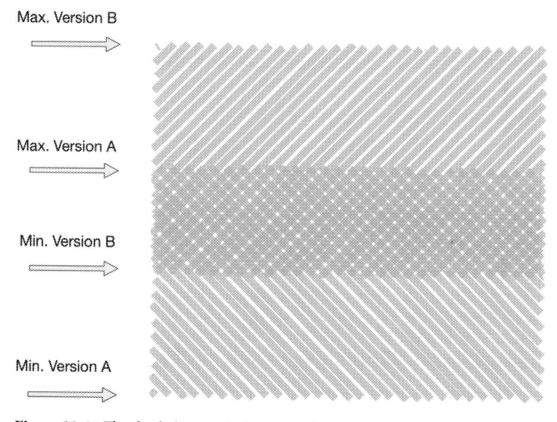

Figure 11-1. *The shaded region is the range of mutually compatible versions*

If two packages both require the same dependency by providing minimum and/or maximum supported version numbers (as shown in Figure 11-1), then we can usually expect to find some range of versions that are mutually compatible. If, instead, one of these packages *pins a specific version,* then it may end up installing this specific version which is outside the compatible range specified by the other package, even if the specific pinned version wasn't necessary.

Source control–based package installation precludes the use of version ranges like this and will *require* version pinning.

Published packaged

For ease of use and consistency installing, as well as visibility and access in the greater Django ecosystem, you'll want to publish your app to a package index. And publishing also allows you to take full advantage of version numbers in requirement specifications, even to a private index.

The very basics of publishing a package include (i) registering the package name on the index, (ii) building the package, and (iii) uploading the build files.

You'll need two additional packages, wheel and twine. The wheel package is used for building Python wheels, which are prebuilt Python packages that are uploaded and downloaded as archive files using the .whl extension. Wheel files are much faster to install for the developer user than a plain source package. The twine package is used for uploading for your package build to the package index. You can do this without twine, but twine will ensure that HTTPS is used and also simplifies the steps of registering and uploading multiple package formats.

```
pip install wheel twine
```

Registering the name is a one-time step that reserves the name of the package. This prevents name conflicts, and so you'll need to make sure your chosen package name hasn't been used yet. However, this is one step we won't take explicitly. You can use the setup.py "register" command; however, it's not necessarily secure, and twine will do this securely and without adding an explicit user step. Nonetheless it's a step worth noting!

In order to take advantage of installing based on version number, your package will need a version number. There are two places we want to include the version number, the setup.py file and your module root. In the case of a standalone Django app, the latter would be myapp/__init__.py. In lieu of a more sophisticated way of propagating version numbers, you can start by hardcoding it both places.

```
# setup.py
from setuptools import setup, find_packages

setup(
    name="blog",
    version="0.1.0",

    author="Ben Lopatin",
    author_email="ben@benlopatin.com",
    url="http://www.django-standalone-apps.com",

    packages=find_packages(exclude=["tests"]),
)
# __init__.py
__version__ = "0.1.0"
```

The version number in your setup.py file is used to register a version number on the package index and to manage the version at installation. The version number included in your package, that is, in the __init__.py file, is helpful metadata to verify what version of the package is installed and in use. This doesn't make it superfluous, but it does mean that changing only the version in the __init__.py file will not, in and of itself, have any material impact on what is published to the package index as a new version. These changes must be made in or through the setup.py file.

> We'll look at some improved ways of handling updates to version
> numbers in Section 4.

Before building and uploading, it's a good idea to quickly check that your package metadata is valid. You can do that by running python setup.py check:

```
python setup.py check -r -s
```

The check command will perform minimal validation on your package metadata. You should always run this step to ensure it's formatted correctly. The -s option will cause the script to exit with an error code if it fails the check, and the -r option checks that all your strings are reStructuredText compliant. You should skip this option if you plan on using Markdown in your README and read into your setup.py file; otherwise this guards against broken formatting on the package index.

With the version number set and the metadata validated, you next need to build a distribution, that is, the file that people will actually download when they install your app. There are, roughly, two ways to build the package: using a source distribution and using a wheel distribution. They are not mutually exclusive, so we'll build both (keeping in mind that you'll need the wheel package installed to build a wheel with the following):

```
python setup.py sdist bdist_wheel
```

This will create an archive with a .whl extension in the dist/ directory of your package and an archive, both named with respect to your package name and version (the particular extension created by sdist varies by system and is configurable).

Then it's time to upload the distributions, and having installed twine, the command looks like this:

```
twine upload dist/*
```

If you haven't registered the package name yet, the twine upload step will do this first before uploading. If it's successful, you'll see your new version – or new package – installed on the package index. If for some reason the upload fails, for example, for only one of the distribution choices, you can fix the problem, if any, and try re-uploading the failed distribution. It's not possible to re-upload a distribution with the same version, but if that distribution wasn't successfully uploaded, then this restriction is inapplicable.

The last step is to tag your release version. With Git you can use the tag command, like so:

```
git tag -a v0.1.0 -m "Initial version"
```

The purpose of tagging is to make sure you can track what exactly was deployed at each version. For this reason you should tag your commits in your repository *after* you have successfully published a new version. This precludes tagging the wrong version if you have to make final changes before uploading the package version.

Summary

In this chapter, you learned some strategies for adding your extracted app back into your project as a standalone app. You learned how to do this locally by installing the app in your project's path, making this work remotely using source control and version tags, and finally by releasing to PyPI as a published installable package. We'll go further into ways of improving the packaging process in subsequent chapters.

PART III

Beyond the Basics

## CHAPTER 12

Handling app settings

Every Django project is configurable by its settings module, its settings.py file. This is how you specify what database you're using and how to connect to it, how to configure your template system, and of course what apps to install. A typical settings file contains a mix of general Django settings (like databases and the secret key), project app settings, and of course settings for standalone apps.

Not every standalone app has a need for its own user configurable settings. But there are all kinds of reasons standalone apps *do* require their own settings, including

1. Third-party API integrations

   • App-specific caching behavior

   • Feature toggling

   • Specifying dependencies

   • Limiting allowed file types

Adding settings to your own project is simple enough, and it's hardly a dark art adding them to a standalone app. However, because the app will be integrated into other projects and likely include settings with various value and type constraints, some forethought is required for naming, structuring, and including these in your app.

Settings naming

The first consideration is naming. Not only should your settings values be clearly named, they should be named so that they're easily associated with your app. In practice this means they should be namespaced with an app-specific prefix.

© Ben Lopatin 2020

B. Lopatin, *Django Standalone Apps*, https://doi.org/10.1007/978-1-4842-5632-9_12

An available example of this can be found in Django itself, in the contrib.auth app. The auth app allows you to specify a custom user model like so:

```
AUTH_USER_MODEL = "custom_users.User"
```

This could easily and more succinctly be named with USER_MODEL, but the AUTH_ preface ensures it's obvious that this corresponds to the auth app.

Thus if your app exposes some settings like this

```
MAX_API_TIMEOUT = 10
SERVICE_API_KEY = "helloworld123"
```

ensure they're namespaced to correspond to your app:

```
MYAPP_MAX_API_TIMEOUT = 10
MYAPP_SERVICE_API_KEY = "helloworld123"
```

Settings formats

Settings are ultimately Python objects accessible via django.conf.settings in a Django project. So while we think of settings like DEBUG with a Boolean value and SECRET_ KEY with a string value, they're not restricted to simple types, or even built-in types. The DATABASES setting is a dictionary, TEMPLATES is a list of dictionaries, and INSTALLED_APPS and MIDDLEWARE are lists of strings.

> *Flat is better than nested.*

In exposing your app's settings for configuration, the simpler the exposed values, the better. In the question of "what format?" the root question is primarily whether to use multiple top-level settings or one or more dictionaries of nested settings.

It may be tempting to use a single dictionary for all of your app's setting values, for instance, so that there's only one "setting." The benefit of this approach is guaranteed simplicity in end users' setting files, but in many instances it can obfuscate the source of these settings. If, for example, an end user is running their Django project using the 12 Factor app style and using environment variables to populate settings values, these should ideally have a 1:1 relationship to a top-level setting value.

> *Although practicality beats purity.*

This should be used as a good default though, and not a hard rule. The primary advantage of exposing settings using dictionaries is that it makes it more obvious when groups of settings are interrelated. In the settings snippet here, it's more readily apparent that the cache settings are tightly related (especially if there are other app settings).

```
MYAPP_CACHE_TTL = 10
MYAPP_CACHE_KEY_PREFIX = "myapp"

MYAPP_CACHE = {
        "TTL": 10,
        "KEY_PREFIX": "myapp",
}
```

However, one drawback of using dictionaries is that it may be less clear how default values are overridden. Does the entire dictionary as provided count as the imported setting? Or are the end user's settings used instead to update existing defaults? At least when a top-level app setting is *not* added in the end user's settings, it is clear that the default will be used.

One final note on the topic of environment variables: I should stress that the use of environment variables in a Django project is the prerogative of the end user, not the standalone app developer. Avoid the temptation to expect values in the process environment and always rely on the settings module. Doing otherwise unnecessarily constrains end users in how they provide their settings, and it also enforces environment variable naming conventions which, though they seem sensible, are not appropriate for the end user's own situation.

Sourcing app settings

The final consideration is how to actually pull these settings into your app where they're needed. This primarily affects your use of the app, as these settings can be expected to mostly be used from within the app itself.

Here's a short example of views.py extract in which several app-specific settings are sources from django.conf.settings:

```
# myapp/views.py

from django.conf import settings
from myapp.client import ApiClient
```

```
USE_CACHING = settings.MYAPP_CACHE_SETTINGS["USE_CACHING"]
CACHE_PREFIX = settings.MYAPP_CACHE_SETTINGS["CACHE_PREFIX"]
CACHE_TTL = settings.MYAPP_CACHE_SETTINGS["CACHE_TTL"]

def list_api_resources(request):
        client = ApiClient(settings.MYAPP_API_KEY)
        api_results = cache.get(f"{CACHE_PREFIX}:results")

        if not api_results:
                api_results = client.list()
                cache.set(f"{CACHE_PREFIX}:results", api_results, CACHE_TTL)

        return render(request, "myapp/api_resources.html", {
                "api_results": api_results,
        })
```

To start with, there are a number of things that could go wrong here:

-   The MYAPP_CACHE_SETTINGS name might not be defined in the settings, or it might be assigned the wrong type, resulting in an AttributeError.

-   The MY_API_KEY could be missing, also resulting in an AttributeError.

-   Similarly, any of the individual MYAPP_CACHE_SETTINGS values might be missing, resulting in a confusing KeyError.

-   And any of the individually provided cache settings might have the wrong type, or wrong *value,* if there are reasonable value bounds for a settings.

In your own project, you can check and bound your settings values in your settings module, but this isn't something you should assume you can delegate to end users of your app. Instead, these should be checked and errors caught within your standalone app as early as possible. In practice what this means is checking for missing or malformed values and raising ImproperlyConfigured errors as soon as possible.

```
# myapp/views.py

from django.conf import settings
from django.core.exceptions import ImproperlyConfigured
```

```python
from myapp.client import ApiClient

if not getattr(settings, "MYAPP_API_KEY"):
        raise ImproperlyConfigured("MYAPP_API_KEY must be set")

try:
        USE_CACHING = settings.MYAPP_CACHE_SETTINGS["USE_CACHING"]
except (AttributeError, KeyError):
        USE_CACHING = False

try:
        CACHE_PREFIX = settings.MYAPP_CACHE_SETTINGS["CACHE_PREFIX"]
except (AttributeError, KeyError):
        USE_CACHING = "myappp"

try:
        CACHE_TTL = int(settings.MYAPP_CACHE_SETTINGS["CACHE_TTL"])
except (AttributeError, KeyError):
        CACHE_TTL = 3600
except (TypeError, ValueError):
        raise ImproperlyConfigured("MYAPP cache TTL must be a number")

def list_api_resources(request):
        """"""

        client = ApiClient(settings.MYAPP_API_KEY)
        api_results = cache.get(f"{CACHE_PREFIX}:results")

        if not api_results:
                api_results = client.list()
                cache.set(f"{CACHE_PREFIX}:results", api_results, CACHE_TTL)

        return render(request, "myapp/api_resources.html", {
                "api_results": api_results,
        }
```

Now at least if an end user forgets to provide MYAPP_API_KEY or accidentally sets the cache TTL to "helloworld", you can catch these errors with comprehensible and helpful error messages. And if a value is missing that can be missing, a sensible default is provided.

However, it is a jumble of code to include in a module with a different purpose, and in the event any of these values are required in other modules, then either this needs to be repeated or those other modules will need to selectively import these cleaned values from your views.py file. Instead, let's move *all* of these app-specific settings into their own module. This will let you encapsulate all of the value checks in one place, and no other module needs to know about how these settings are sourced or given.

An obvious name for such a module is settings.py although conf.py and app_settings. py are also common choices. My own preference is for conf.py. The first is the most popular route to take, and while sensible, it means it's more likely to cause confusion, especially in the event any other module in your app imports django.conf.settings; of course a solution to that is to simply import *those* individually needed global settings into your app settings module.

Now with an app-specific settings module from which these can be imported from, the views.py and other modules only need to import it and can avoid any kind of additional error and default value handling:

```
# myapp/conf.py

from django.conf import settings
from django.core.exceptions import ImproperlyConfigured

# Required values

MYAPP_API_KEY = getattr(settings, "MYAPP_API_KEY")
if not MYAPPP_API_KEY:
        raise ImproperlyConfigured("MYAPP_API_KEY is missing")

# Values with defaults

USE_CACHING = True
CACHE_PREFIX = "myapp"
CACHE_TTL = 60 * 60

try:
        USE_CACHING = settings.MYAPP_CACHE_SETTINGS["USE_CACHING"]
except (AttributeError, KeyError):
        pass
```

```
try:
        CACHE_PREFIX = settings.MYAPP_CACHE_SETTINGS["CACHE_PREFIX"]
except (AttributeError, KeyError):
        pass

try:
        CACHE_TTL = int(settings.MYAPP_CACHE_SETTINGS["CACHE_TTL"])
except (AttributeError, KeyError):
        pass
except (TypeError, ValueError):
        raise ImproperlyConfigured("MYAPP cache TTL must be a number")
```

Summary

In this chapter, we walked through strategies for handling app-specific settings, including how to namespace and structure app-specific settings, how to source them in your app, and how to best handle missing and bad values.

In the next chapter, we'll look at how to make your standalone app useable in languages other than your own.

CHAPTER 13

Internationalization

Internationalization and localization allow applications to be used by people in different languages and using different written contexts (e.g., date formats). Conceptually simple, it's a powerful way to make software available to more people.

As a native English speaker in a predominantly English-speaking country, I think it's fair to say that most native English speakers in English-speaking countries give little thought to how their software will be used by people who speak other languages or by those in other countries. However, writing software for only one language "market" works against your benefit since the cost to you to make the software available in other languages is fairly low, and the consequence is a larger user base, both end users and potential contributors.

There are several steps to making your standalone Django app useful to speakers of other languages, which are simultaneously sequential and in order of priority.

Why translation

As a simple example, let's assume your app includes a form class that performs some basic validation. In our case, it checks to see if the value provided in the coupon field matches a currently active Coupon. If it doesn't, then the data does not validate, and an error string is returned with the form to be displayed to the user.

```
class CouponForm(forms.Form):
    coupon = forms.CharField(required=False)

        def clean_coupon(self):
                data = self.cleaned_data.get('coupon', '')
                if data and not Coupon.objects.active().filter(code=data).
                exists():
```

© Ben Lopatin 2020
B. Lopatin, *Django Standalone Apps*, https://doi.org/10.1007/978-1-4842-5632-9_13

```
                    raise forms.ValidationError(
                            "Invalid coupon code"
                    )
            return data
```

Now for every user of your app, the validation message displayed will always be "You have entered an invalid coupon code" regardless of what language(s) they have their site configured for. If you wanted to provide this in Spanish, instead, you'd need to check for the field or specific message in your Django project and then return a custom message.

```
class CouponView(FormView):

    def form_invalid(self, form):
        context = super().get_context_data(form=form)
        spanish_errors = {}
        if (
                form.errors.get("coupon", [""])[0] ==
                "Invalid coupon code"
        ):
                spanish_errors["coupon"] = "Cupón inválido"
        context["spanish_errors"] = spanish_errors
        return self.render_to_response(context)
```

This is obviously a contrived example which you can probably see some ways to simplify already. But it would be nice if such custom changes where wholly unnecessary. And with a few minor tweaks, they are unnecessary.

Translatable strings and how translation works

The solution can be implemented wholly in the form class with one import and "wrapping" the string in a function call to gettext:

```
from django.utils.translation import gettext as _

class CouponForm(forms.Form):
    coupon = forms.CharField(required=False)
```

```
def clean_coupon(self):
    data = self.cleaned_data.get('coupon', '')
    if data and not Coupon.objects.active().filter(code=data).
    exists():
        raise forms.ValidationError(
            _("Invalid coupon code")
        )
    return data
```

I'll call it "wrapping" the string because using the common _ alias that's what it looks like, but make no mistake about it, this is a function call. When executed, the string returned will be sourced by using the external program gettext based on the locale set in the calling context, which will either be the default locale or the locale chosen by the end user in their session.

In this manner internationalization is nothing more than a simple dictionary lookup. Unlike an English-Spanish dictionary, however, there are no subtle options for a chosen word or phrase; rather this lookup behaves more like a Python dictionary where every string is an exact key that returns another string.

A common objection to internationalization is that the original developer doesn't know what the potential languages are or know them well enough to provide translations, so there's little point in making the effort. Fortunately, there are no such requirements to making standalone apps translatable, or even translated!

Prioritizing translation steps

The first step in enabling translation is making your strings translatable. At its simplest, this means "wrapping" your strings in a call to one of the gettext functions as previously described. There are a couple of gettext functions in the django.utils. translation module, as well as a template tag library; their detailed use is documented in the official Django documentation and unnecessary to cover here. **The number one priority in your app is ensuring that user-facing strings in Python code are "wrapped" with** gettext **and translatable**. If you do nothing else but this, you'll have accomplished that critical 80%.

The reason this is the singular priority is twofold: one, it is entirely possible to create the necessary language files for any language given that the strings are available for lookup, and two, this is the only user-facing content that the end developer cannot change.

> By user-facing strings, I mean here any string that would be expected to be displayed to the application user and seen in their browser. Unless an exception is used to raise a message to the end user (e.g., via a validation error), you probably don't want to translate exception messages.

Making templates translatable is the second priority, and whether this is a close or distant second will depend entirely on the nature of templates in your Django standalone app. The reason here is that templates are entirely extendable and overridable by developer users. If your templates are sparse and fully intended to be replaced by developers, then the value of making these translatable is negligible. On the other hand, if the templates in your application are richly structured and intended to be part of the user-facing experience, then making sure these are translatable – by using the template tags from the i18n tag library – should be high priority.

With these two tasks out of the way, the necessity and value of further efforts now steeply decline unless you have known use cases in specific languages and ready resources for creating translations. Those additional steps include generating and adding po files, the text-based source files for `gettext` translations, integrating with a translations service, and compiling and including mo files, the binary lookup files used by `gettext`.

Generating and adding po files is simple enough and requires absolutely no knowledge of the target language. However, it *does* involve choosing a language! This is a bit like optimizing without measuring. Until you know what demand there is for specific languages, you're in no position to make this choice. It might make it more obvious that your app is ready for translation *contributions,* but even this is a suspect strategy. Of the three most widely spoken languages in the Western Hemisphere, there are numerous country-specific varieties; and where translations are used, these otherwise small differences are often significant.

Model content and translations

There are several sources of user-facing content in a Django application: from the templates, from the Python code itself, and from user-controlled model-based content. In most websites and web applications with non-trivial amounts of content, model-based content makes up the bulk of the content. While you as the standalone app author are not providing this content, you can provide affordances for developer users to add translations. Of course, how you do this and whether it's necessary or valuable depend on the nature of your standalone app.

In your own Django project, using models you control, there are several solutions available, beyond those described in the following. Third-party standalone apps like [django-modeltranslation] (`https://django-modeltranslation.readthedocs.io/en/latest/registration.html`) let you add locale-specific fields to existing models and access these seamless from your app with minimal intervention. However, this involves modifying database tables, which means database migrations, and in the case of third-party apps, this means trying to manage migrations for a library not under your control and moreover losing track of these migrations if you're using any kind of ephemeral deployment system, all of which is to say that for the developer user managing a Django project, trying to add translation support to the models in third-party apps is not viable. Thankfully, there *are* affordances you can provide as the developer of a Django standalone app.

For a content heavy application, where a model has several or numerous fields representing user-facing content, an excellent and flexible strategy is to include a locale field and allow translations to vary by instance or, more specifically, by database row. This means that for an Email model, for instance, you might allow multiple instances with the same base:

```
from django.conf import settings
from django.db import models

class EmailType:
        confirmation = "confirmation"
        notification = "notification"

        @classmethod
        def choices(cls):
                return [(cls.notification, cls.notification),
                                (cls.confirmation, cls.confirmation)]
```

```
class EmailMessage(models.Model):
        email_type = models.CharField(
                max_length=20,
                choices=EmailType.choices(),
        )
        locale = models.CharField(
                max_length=10,
                choices=settings.LANGUAGES,
                default="",
        )
        message = models.TextField()

        class Meta:
                unique_together = ("email_type", "locale")
```

Now there's a built-in way to include translated content in the database, without any further modification of the database. This strategy makes the most sense for "content heavy" models, though, that represent either a significant amount of content or a large number of fields that should all be translated together.

For models with only a few fields requiring translation, another option, and one that has not been pursued to much fanfare as of this writing, is to make use of built-in lookup fields. If you're willing to commit your developer users to the PostgreSQL database, then using either the HStoreField or JSONField is an option. Both can be used to represent dictionaries; HStoreField is simpler and restricted to strings, but JSONField uses default database functionality (HStoreField requires that you install a database extension).

Taking this strategy to its maximum potential is an encouraged exercise for the reader, but at its simplest it involves storing core field data in a dictionary:

```
from django.contrib.postgres.fields import JSONField
from django.db import models

class Product(models.Model):
        title_source = JSONField()
        price = models.IntegerField()
```

```
def title(self, locale=""):
    if locale:
        try:
            return self.title_source[locale]
        except KeyError:
            pass
    return self.title_source[""]
```

This neatly solves for the data storage problem, as well as explicit retrieval. The usability of such an interface warrants vast improvement, including for updating data and especially for the simplified querying as afforded by something like django-translation. Maybe that could be your first Django standalone app!

Summary

In this chapter, we reviewed what internationalization is and why it's important to accommodate in your standalone app. You learned how to prioritize adding translation support to your app, when to include specific language translations for your app, and also how to approach translating model-based content.

In the next chapter, we'll learn about the problems of managing version compatibility with different Python and Django versions and some strategies for solving these problems.

## CHAPTER 14

Managing version compatibility

When you write a Django app to include in your own project, you have known versions of Python, Django, and every other dependency used. When you create a standalone app, you have neither knowledge nor control over these versions since this will be deployed in other people's projects. As a result what "works for me" may turn out not to work in even subtlety different environments for other developers. You may not be able to know exactly which versions every user and prospective user have deployed, but you can anticipate major combinations of Python, Django, and even dependency versions and ensure that your app works in each. This has the added bonus of making upgrades easier for you wherever you use your own standalone app.

The critical tools here are strategies for testing these version differences and strategies for simultaneously supporting different possibly incompatible versions of Python, Django, and additional library dependencies.

Python version

Differences in Python version may seem like the gnarliest of version differences to address, but with the end of official support for Python 2, the practical differences that most standalone apps will need to address are no longer quite so significant. That said, there will be cases where you find functionality that works in one Python version, but not in another. Python's f-strings, for example, were added in Python 3.6, and if your goal is to *fully* support Django 2.2 as a long-term support release, then you'd need to support Python 3.5. Thus f-strings should be replaced with standard string formatting. Similarly assignment expressions, colloquially known as the walrus operator, were added only added in Python 3.8, so their use in your standalone app precludes anyone running Python 3.7 from using your app.

B. Lopatin, *Django Standalone Apps*, https://doi.org/10.1007/978-1-4842-5632-9_14

This gets to the primary question you'll need to address regarding Python versions, that is, which versions to support. If the cost of supporting additional versions is low, it's good to err on the side of supporting these versions. This could mean another version number of Python or other interpreters. The majority of deployments assuredly run on CPython, but it's not the only way to run Python. As of this writing, the only major alternative implementation that supports Python 3 is PyPy, a JIT compiler; Jython and IronPython, Java, and .NET runtime implementations only support up to Python 2.7.

Testing against different versions of Python works much like one would expect – setting up version-unique virtual environments and running the tests in each:

```
$ python3.6 -m venv venvs/python36
$ source venvs/python36/bin/activate
$ python setup.py install
$ ./runtests.py
$ python3.7 -m venv venvs/python37
$ source venvs/python3.7/bin/activate
$ python setup.py install
$ ./runtests.py
$ python3.8 -m venv venvs/python38
$ source venvs/python3.8/bin/activate
$ python setup.py install
$ ./runtests.py
```

This, however, would quickly become tedious and error prone. Instead, we can replace the entire structure and process with the testing tool tox, like so:

```
$ pip install tox
$ tox
```

First, we'll need a minimal tox.ini configuration file so that tox knows what environments to create and what to install in them:

```
[tox]
envlist = py36, py37, py38
```

```
[testenv]
setenv =
    PYTHONPATH = {toxinidir}:{toxinidir}/myapp
commands = python runtests.py
basepython =
    py36: python3.6
    py37: python3.7
    py38: python3.8
deps =
    -r{toxinidir}/requirements.txt
```

This file has two component blocks, tox and testenv. The first is where we declare the default environments. These will be created, if they do not exist, and tests run in them every time tox is run without environments specified.

The second block for testenv is where we specify what goes into the test environments, how to run the tests, and where we specify the Python versions. Each item described in basepython should correspond to an executable name. This is also where you would include alternative Python implementations:

```
basepython =
        pypy: pypy
    py36: python3.6
    py37: python3.7
    py38: python3.8
```

The other item to point out here is the deps configuration. This allows you to specify which dependencies are installed and in which environments. For this base example, we'll assume that all app and testing dependencies are defined in a requirements.txt file, from which each will be installed in the respective tox environment when the tool is run.

Django and dependencies

The most obvious and practically important version difference you'll need to concern yourself with is different Django versions. Major version changes bring deprecations and breaking changes, and running your standalone app with a different version of Django than you originally tested it against may result in unexpected errors.

A word about version pinning: While it's a good idea to include
Django as a requirement for your standalone app, be careful
about being overly aggressive about setting version boundaries.
Upper boundaries should only be set when there's a known
incompatibly between the current version of your standalone
app and a released or soon-to-be released version. Lower
boundaries similarly should represent safety from known and
unsupported version issues. If you decide not to support a lower
version of Django, setting a minimum version requirement will
help ensure developer users are using only known-to-be-working
environment with your app. It also means that even if it happens
to work for that version of Django that someone else needs to use,
they won't be able to.

The primary question you'll face is which versions to test and support. Absent any
special requirements from your own projects that would demand features in newer
versions, a good rule of thumb is to target Django versions supported by the Django
open source project itself. That means the latest release and current long-term support
releases. At the start of 2020, this would mean Django 3.0 and 2.2 (LTS).

You may face similar issues if your standalone app has outside dependencies on
other Django apps. Here things may become more complicated if these apps do not offer
similar version coverage.

In the Figure 14-1, we compare three different dependencies (helpfully named A, B,
and C) with their own range of Django version support. If each of these dependencies
is required, then your own standalone app's supported versions are bounded by their
supported Django versions, represented by the dotted line.

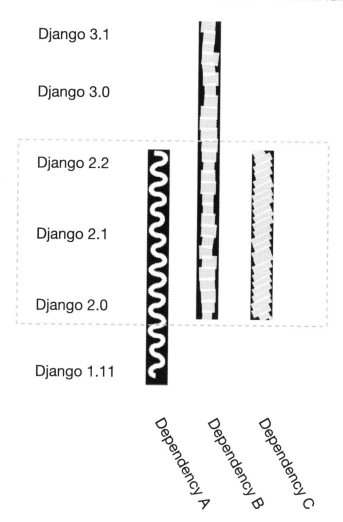

Django 3.1

Django 3.0

Django 2.2

Django 2.1

Django 2.0

Django 1.11

Dependency A

Dependency B

Dependency C

Figure 14-1. *The range of compatible Django versions*

You may also run into an issue where Dependency C, for example, only supports Django 3.0 and above and Dependency A only supports up through Django 2.2 but as optional dependencies, rather than required dependencies.f. If such an incompatibility arises, the main recourse you'll have is documenting the version combinations that must be used in combination. This scenario is unlikely to arise but can when supporting optional features in the app.

Solving for incompatibilities

Changes in APIs require conditional feature naming and importing. *Likely* this means trying to get the proper names imported multiple times across multiple modules in your standalone app, whether or not these are the same name. The problem with this is not that it won't work, but that it clutters your modules and tends to require code duplication.

The solution is to combine all of your feature and version-conditional imports and definitions into a single module, much like was achieved for app settings.

```
try:
        from django.urls import reverse
except ImportError:
        from django.core.urlresolvers import reverse

try:
        from third_party.lib import cool_function
except ImportError:
        from third_party.utils import cool_function
```

A common convention is to simply include these in a compat.py module. Historically this was critical for supporting both Python 2 and Python 3, but you may find it necessary for differences in Django versions, third-party dependencies, and, yes, even Python versions.

If necessary, don't be afraid to vendor. This could be copying an individual function or even a module wholesale if it's critical to your standalone app but not available in one of the versions of Django or other dependencies that you want to support. Remember to include and abide by all licensing terms when you do this.

Future proofing

Even if you decide there are no feature updates you want to make to your app after publishing it, you may find that it makes use of Django features that become depreciated. The foundation for ensuring that your app continues to work with new versions of Django (and Python) is continually testing with the latest versions of Django and Python, even unreleased or unsupported versions.

A basic tox file as follows is designed to test two different LTS versions of Django and also the (hypothetical) pre-release version 4.0a1. Pre-release packages can be published to PyPI and downloaded using their pinned version, but are not installable using ranges. The downside is that you may need to update this as subsequent pre-release versions are published.

```
[tox]
envlist = py37, py38

[testenv]
setenv =
    PYTHONPATH = {toxinidir}:{toxinidir}
commands = python runtests.py
basepython =
    py37: python3.7
    py38: python3.8
deps =
        django22: Django>=2.2,<3
    django32: Django>=3.2,<4
        django40: Django==4.0a1
    -r{toxinidir}/requirements-test.txt
```

Summary

In this chapter, you learned about the challenges posed by supporting different versions of Python and Django, dependency scope issues when using additional dependencies, and strategies for solving these issues. These solutions include relying on dedicated compatibility modules as well as rigorously testing against combinations of Python and Django versions.

In the next chapter, we'll look into providing multiple framework and backend targets for apps that go beyond supporting Django.

CHAPTER 15

Mixed dependency support

In the previous chapter, you learned how to manage version compatibility between your app and different versions of Python and Django. In this chapter, we'll look beyond Django and toward offering feature compatibility with both Django and other non-Django-related libraries.

Beyond Django

The functionality in a Django app, even a "standalone" app, is not required to ship in a Django-only package. You may find that the core functionality you want to extract or include in a standalone Django app is largely not Django-specific and, further, that you'd like to make that core functionality available outside of Django projects. This leaves with you a couple of choices. One would be to create a distinct base package, one that is Django or generally framework agnostic, and then a separate Django-specific package. This is a perfectly valid strategy. The second strategy would be to create a single package that includes Django-specific functionality, or even that for other frameworks, as separate `contrib` modules that ship with your package.

For cases where the framework-specific functionality, that is, the bundled Django standalone app, is primarily a framework adapter for the core and framework-agnostic functionality, the second strategy should simplify development and package maintenance. The "downside" of shipping a module that someone might not use should be considered minimal, especially compared to the costs of maintaining separate packages and increasing the dependency requirements for other developer users.

© Ben Lopatin 2020
B. Lopatin, *Django Standalone Apps*, https://doi.org/10.1007/978-1-4842-5632-9_15

The nuts and bolts

Consider an advanced *lorem ipsum* generator. *Lorem ipsum* is the pseudo Latin text used frequently by designers to fill in the content areas of designs, including websites, so that other stakeholders can get a feel for the design when the final content is unavailable, for example:

> Lorem ipsum dolor sit amet, consectetur adipiscing elit, sed do
> eiusmod tempor incididunt ut labore et dolore magna aliqua.

Django even ships with a built-in template tag, lorem, that will generate this text:

```
{% lorem 5 p %}
```

But you've decided to go beyond this, to allow your team or anyone to be able to generate *lorem*-like placeholder text from a different and tag-specific corpus, including tech buzzwords, MBA jargon, and hipster-lorem.

The solution is obviously implemented with a new template tag, which you call lorem_plus, and has a similar interface to the built-in lorem tag:

```
{% lorem_plus 'hipster' 1 %}
```

This returns some placeholder text from the specified corpus:

> Taxidermy meditation humblebrag, stumptown migas messenger
> bag slow-carb.

And while the implementation required to use this in a Django project is Django specific – Django template tags are more or less useless anywhere else – the core functionality is pretty general. This involves selecting a corpus, assembling some "sentences," packing these into paragraphs of one format or another, and then optionally wrapping the output (e.g., as safe markup). It would be quite useful for Jinja templates, too, whether in a Django project or a Flask project.

This can be accomplished by segmenting not just the Django template-specific code from Jinja-specific code, but from the core functionality itself. Instead of having a structure like this

```
templatetags/
        __init__.py
        lorem_tags.py
__init__.py
```

the package module might have a structure like this:

```
templatetags/
        __init__.py
        lorem_tags.py
__init__.py
core.py
jinja_tags.py
```

The core.py module would have all of the "business logic," including the lorem generating function, lorem_generator, which returns the base string which each template implementation can then mark as safe for rendering. Here could be our function signature (the body is omitted as unnecessary for our purposes here):

```
# core.py
def lorem_generator(corpus, count=1, method="b"):
        """

        Returns randomized placeholder text

        Args:

                corpus: string identifying the corpus
                count: number of words or paragraphs
                method: words 'w', HTML paragraphs 'p',
                        or plaintext paragraphs 'b'

        Returns: a string
        """
```

Then all that's required for the template backend implementations is to call this function and return the string marked safe for rendering, for Django:

```
# lorem_tags.py
@register.tag
def lorem_plus(corpus, count=1, method="b"):
        placeholder = lorem_generator(corpus, count, method)
        return mark_safe(placeholder)
```

And for Jinja:

```
# jinja_tags.py
def lorem_plus(corpus, count=1, method="b"):
        placeholder = lorem_generator(corpus, count, method)
        return jinja2.Markup(placeholder)
```

Now, the same functionality can be used across not just template backends but frameworks, as the Django feature in the app is only an implementation detail of the core functionality.

Real-world examples

This particular scenario is not very common, though it is quite useful.

WhiteNoise is a *static file* serving utility, designed to simplify serving static files in production websites. It's a Python package that supports the same WSGI (Web Server Gateway Interface) protocol that Django relies on to interface with a production application server. As such it can be used with any WSGI application, Django or otherwise. However, there *are* certain affordances for Django that allow integrating WhiteNoise within the Django project, rather than at the WSGI level, making for convenient integration in development, the collectstatic management command for pre-release tasks, and middleware.

All of these features can be supported by including this functionality in modules that are not required, that is, not imported, by any of the core functionality. In order to simplify using WhiteNoise in development – which is otherwise enabled by passing --nostatic to the runserver management command – you can add an included Django app to your project's INSTALLED_APPS list.

```
INSTALLED_APPS = [
    'whitenoise.runserver_nostatic',
    'django.contrib.staticfiles',
    # everything else
]
```

The runserver_nostatic app is, functionally, nothing more than a single management command which extends the runserver command. However, combined with the included middleware, it enables all of the functionality of WhiteNoise to be used seamlessly within a Django project and without compromising the usefulness of the core functionality for someone using it with Flask.

That's a real-world example of including some minor adaptations or integrations from generalized functionality into a Django project. As should take little motivation to see now, this can also be done with more deeply integrated functionality.

nplusone is a utility for "detecting the n+1 queries problem in Python ORMs." This is one of the most common database-related performance problems in ORM-based applications, in which returning a list (queryset) of some model from the database results not in one query but in one query for every single item returned plus the original query. It's a result of fetching attributes from related models and in Django apps is most often simply solved by using select_related or prefetch_related. However, this isn't a Django-specific problem, and nplusone supports the major Python ORMs in one package, including Django, SQLAlchemy, and Peewee.

The major problem here is not simply providing some minor adaptions of the core functionality. Instead, each supported ORM requires its own set of unique features. The base or core module provides some common "scaffolding"-like exceptions and signal management, but the ORM-specific implementations are unique.

The natural question is why not ship these as separate packages then? Without speaking for the maintainer, it does offer simpler development and maintenance, not to mention project marketing. And probably more importantly, or specifically, it allows capturing *domain-specific changes* across implementations. A release that adds checks for unused data attributes in queries, motivated by a problem that isn't specific to any one ORM, lends itself to release across each implementation in a single new version, rather than a series of individual releases for the same domain feature.

Summary

In this chapter, you learned how to separate Django-specific and backend-specific features from more general features to allow reusing app functionality outside of Django projects and/or with different backing classes (e.g., template backends). You learned that you can separate functionality into different published packages or simply make use of alternate modules within your published package to simplify development while keeping your library extensible. In the next chapter, you'll learn what horizontal and vertical modularity mean and how these two segmentation paradigms can be used to help organize your app.

CHAPTER 16

Modularity

We break Django projects into apps to segment by *horizontal* programming functionality and *vertical* business features to make them easier to work with and reason about, and of course so these components are easier to reuse.

Some of these segments are more tightly defined than others, resulting in smaller and/or more narrowly written apps. Compare, for example, django-model-utils and django-extensions. Both offer some overlapping features in the form of helpful model and field classes, but django-model-utils has a primary focus on solving for repeated model-related functionality, and django-extensions has a primary focus on solving more general features which are useful across Django projects, and happens to include such model-related functionality. It's not that one is better than the other; rather the scope of each stems from the problem area for which it's solving.

This is to say that some problem areas lend themselves to broader scopes, even when the problem can be concisely defined. "Managing user-created content on a website" is a nicely defined business problem, but in practice includes a variety of non-trivial sub-requirements. Further, these sub-requirements – like managing multimedia or user-specific content – may not be required in a plurality of use cases.

This leads to decisions about whether and how to further modularize your standalone app, including using sub-apps and yet additional standalone apps.

Additional standalone apps

Breaking a larger standalone app into yet further standalone apps would be *apropos*. It's a way of further segmenting the app, for examples, by vertical business feature, so that the subcomponents are tightly focused. It has its uses but also some costs especially as a primary strategy.

© Ben Lopatin 2020
B. Lopatin, *Django Standalone Apps*, https://doi.org/10.1007/978-1-4842-5632-9_16

The benefits of pursuing this strategy and breaking a larger standalone app into component standalone apps track with the benefits of creating a standalone app in the first place. The separated apps can be developed, tested, and reused with smaller codebases, allowing users to install only the components they need for their projects.

This strategy has some obvious and less than obvious drawbacks however.

First, maintaining separate packages has decreasing marginal value and increasing marginal cost for the maintainer. A backward incompatible or breaking change in the core app means parallel changes must be orchestrated across the component apps and parallel releases, too. This work is easier when all of the changes can be orchestrated within a single package, taking better advantage of refactoring tools and a common test of tests.

Second, it begs the question that the core app – which we're presuming here – is sufficiently useful on its own. There certainly could be value in having a core app that is little more than a commonly used foundation package, but if that's the case, then most likely it's not so much a standalone app on its own so much as a useful foundational package to use with separate standalone apps.

Third, this is extra hassle for your developer users. There are benefits to using more granular dependencies like not including code you don't need, which may cause unwanted deployment bloat, or exposure to extraneous bugs and compatibility issues. It also adds more individual dependencies to track.

When this strategy should be taken up is when the secondary functionality is expected to be opt in, and of a plug in nature, when the functionality may have non-trivial use cases absent the core app such that it's useful as an installed package on its own, or when its management is better decoupled from the core app. If the subcomponent benefits from a faster release cycle, this may be the case. Where the package coupling would otherwise make it easier to keep subcomponents in sync with core, it now would likely hold back valuable releases for the subcomponents.

An example of this decoupling is django-localflavor which was formerly django.contrib.localflavor. As a repository of country-specific utilities, like lists of states and provinces, and form and model field which validate postal codes and phone numbers, it functions as much as a knowledge repository as it does functional library. Separating out this subcomponent allows a separation of focus from programmatic utilities of the framework and locale-specific knowledge accrual.

Using sub-apps

A viable and well-traveled alternative path to creating separate standalone apps is to break up your standalone app into sub-apps which are all included in the main package. This is the strategy employed by nearly every Django-based CMS, including Wagtail, Django CMS, and Mezzanine. And of course Django itself ships multiple related apps in one consolidated package, django.contrib.

The django.contrib example is both an exception to how this works and illustrative. It's an exception because of course it ships with the very framework, but also there isn't truly a single "core" app, for example, you can't add django.contrib to your INSTALLED_ APPS. There is a network of dependence in the django.contrib; contrib.auth, contrib. admin, and contrib.sites all require contrib.contenttypes, but each solves for a generally unrelated business requirement.

Despite aiming at different business requirements, these apps are frequently used together, hence their common packaging. They do not all need to be installed in your project's INSTALLED_APPS apps, and the presence of the unused apps is of little downside as a developer user.

When your subcomponents are separate installable apps, they need to be individually installed to be used as apps (e.g., using models, templates, template tags):

```
INSTALLED_APPS = [
        "myapp",
        "myapp.virtual_reality",
        "myapp.augmented_reality",
        ...
]
```

Embracing horizontal modularity

If in fact there is no obvious way of subdividing a very large app into vertically segmented subcomponents by sub-feature, you can always fall back on "horizontal" segmentation. Once again, this mean organizing code along programmatic utility as opposed to business requirement or feature (vertical).

```
myapp/
        forms/
                ...
        models/
                __init__.py
                augmented_reality_models.py
                core_models.py
                virtual_reality_models.py
        ...
```

If nothing else, such a pattern is better than a contrived attempt at vertical segmentation where no clear business feature divide exists.

For most *new* standalone apps though, all of these questions will be more hypothetical than real.

Summary

In this chapter, you learned about the importance of modularity in your standalone app and the ramifications of different code organization schemes for both code reuse and legibility for other developers. In the next chapter, we'll return to the issue of packaging and learn how to better track package versions, ensure your tests run against installable code, and configure your project to create package index-ready releases.

CHAPTER 17

Better packaging

In Chapter 8 we took a Django app and created a simple Python package to distribute that app. What we're after here is simpler package configuration code, that is, easier to read and simpler to update, as well as maximal assurance that what we test is what we ship.

In this chapter, we revisit our package from Chapter 8 and explore some ways to improve upon the package we set up in order to include additional information and to make updating that information easier.

Version consolidation

Our setup.py file in Chapter 8 looked like this:

```python
from setuptools import setup, find_packages

setup(
    name="blog",
    version="0.1.0",
    author="Ben Lopatin",
    author_email="ben@benlopatin.com",
    url="http://www.django-standalone-apps.com",
    packages=find_packages(exclude=["tests"]),
)
```

The package version is specified here as a string in the setup file. We need the version included here in order to inform the package index of the specific version. The problem with using a string literal as we have here is that you'll end up with this string repeated

© Ben Lopatin 2020
B. Lopatin, *Django Standalone Apps*, https://doi.org/10.1007/978-1-4842-5632-9_17

throughout. If you include the version in your package itself, as you should, then you have two places you need to update the version every time you update for a release.

> The benefit of having the version defined within your package, for example, as a variable set in your __init__.py file, is that it is always available for verifying the version from other packages. It's trivial, for example, to open up a Python console, import the package, and check what the value of myapp.__version__ is.

The crux of the solution is to include the version in one canonical location and reuse it elsewhere. There are a few ways to do this which ultimately rely on treating your module root – that is, __init__.py or a specialized file – as the source of truth.

The most obvious strategy is to simply declare the version in your __init__.py file like so

```
__version__ = "2.4.0"
```

and then import the package in your setup.py file

```
from setuptools import setup, find_packages

import myapp

setup(
    name="blog",
    version=myapp.__version__,
    author="Ben Lopatin",
    author_email="ben@benlopatin.com",
    url="http://www.django-standalone-apps.com",
    packages=find_packages(exclude=["tests"]),
)
```

It is an appealing strategy but also one that should be avoided. Importing the package that is being installed, before it is installed, can pose problems during installation, especially if your app specifies any dependencies that are only installed by your app. An alternative is to use a separate module only for package metadata, from which it is safe to import the version. Let's call it __meta__.py:

```
__version__ = "2.4.0"
__author__ = "Ben Lopatin"
```

Your __init__.py file can import the values from this __meta__.py file, and your setup.py can, too, without risk or importing uninstalled dependencies.

```
from setuptools import setup, find_packages

import myapp.__meta__

setup(
    name="blog",
    version=myapp.__meta__.__version__,
    author=myapp.__meta__.__author__,
    author_email="ben@benlopatin.com",
    url="http://www.django-standalone-apps.com",
    packages=find_packages(exclude=["tests"]),
)
```

A proven alternative to importing these values is to read and parse the file without even importing it into the namespace. The value of this strategy will show itself shortly.

```
from setuptools import setup, find_packages

with open("myapp/__init__.py", "r") as module_file:
    for line in module_file:
        if line.startswith("__version__"):
            version_string = line.split("=")[1]
            version = version_string.strip().replace("\"", "")

setup(
    name="blog",
    version=version,
    author="Ben Lopatin",
    author_email="ben@benlopatin.com",
    url="http://www.django-standalone-apps.com",
    packages=find_packages(exclude=["tests"]),
)
```

This entertains no risk of importing modules and can be done even when the code itself is *not yet importable.*

Using a source directory

In our basic package example (Chapter 8), the source directory looked like this:

```
blog_app
├── blog/
├── ...
├── manage.py
├── runtests.py
├── setup.py
|── tests/
|── ...
```

where blog/ represents the *package directory* for the code. When installed, the packaged contents of blog will be available using import blog. This is the most natural way of packing a Python app, but it has one significant drawback.

> Your tests do not run against the package as it will be installed by its users. They run against whatever the situation in your project directory is.[1]

Regardless of the code layout you use, one problem you may encounter is that you may end up running your tests against code that differs from what you publish to the package index. It could be because of changes to your local repository that you haven't committed or files that are not included in your repository. *That* problem is easily solved by running tests automatically using a continuous integration system.

The problem entailed by the directory layout is similar enough but deviously different. It's possible to run the tests against the exact same files present in the published repository and yet have them miss errors in the deployed code because what is in your package *directory* is not necessarily what is *installed* by the package! Based on how you defined both the packages parameter and what you define in your MANIFEST. in file, you may end up with different – that is, missing – source code in the installed version.

The goal of putting this source code in your src/ directory is that it enforces testing against only installed code in order to reduce the likelihood that you ship a broken or incomplete package.

---

[1]Hynek Schlawack, `https://hynek.me/articles/testing-packaging/`

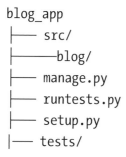

```
blog_app
├── src/
├────blog/
├── manage.py
├── runtests.py
├── setup.py
├── tests/
```

This works due to several factors. The first is that the src/ directory is not a Python module. It includes only your code package(s), it does not include its own __init__. py file. This precludes importing from the package directory directly. Second, the tests are in their own top-level module rather than located inside the package directory. This enforces running the tests against the installed package, and not the code in your directory.

Despite the benefits for package releases, moving the code to a separate directory brings with it a few minor challenges. The first is that you can no longer run your tests directly! Your app code is not in your Python path any longer. Using tox or nox to test in isolated test-specific virtual environments solves several problems, including allowing you to reinstall the app in isolation for test runs. A more immediate though less reliable strategy is to add the src/ directory to your path.

```
PYTHONPATH=src/ pytest tests
```

This method is convenient for development, but should not be depended on for releases since it circumvents the protections afforded by moving the code to the src/ directory.

One of the challenges of moving our code with a Django standalone app is that we want to use the code to create artifacts that are included in the source code and in the package. If we wanted to use a manage.py script to create migrations for the standalone app, we'd run into the same problem with testing in place. Thankfully this can be resolved using similar strategies as with testing. Here it makes more sense to use the simple path modified command:

```
PYTHONPATH=src/ ./manage.py makemigrations myapp
```

Creating migrations – and any other app-specific tasks – can also be encapsulated in a tox environment or nox session, simply for convenience or to ensure that such tasks are running against the installed package:

```
@nox.session
def migrate_on_path(session):
    session.install("-r", "requirements-test.txt")
    env = {"PYTHONPATH": "src/"}
    session.run("python", "manage.py", "check", env=env)
    session.run(
                "python", "manage.py", "makemigrations", "myapp", env=env)

@nox.session
def migrate_from_installed(session):
        session.install("-e", ".")
    session.run("python", "manage.py", "check", env=env)
    session.run(
                "python", "manage.py", "makemigrations", "myapp", env=env)
```

Each of these "sessions" will run in its own isolated virtual environment. The first will run the check command and build migrations against the source as laid out in your src/ directory. This session would need to install any requirements otherwise added when you install your app or expected to be installed, for example, Django itself. The second nox "session" installs the app and then executes the commands against the installed package.

Using setup.cfg

Removing the version from the setup.py file as a string literal is a quality improvement, reducing the likelihood of versioning errors in your package. There are additional improvements that can be made in your package configuration that make it easier to read and update.

Instead of providing all of the metadata as arguments to the setup function in your setup.py file, you can instead add these in a more readable ini-formatted setup.cfg file. There are several benefits to doing this instead, aside from readability. One is that the file can be used for other tools' metadata (e.g., linting tools), and secondly it provides a

native strategy for extracting the version from a module attribute. Provided that
__version__ is the version identifier and it's defined in or imported in the __init__.py file,
the following example setup.cfg file will adequately replace the metadata definition in
our setup.py file:

```
[metadata]
name = blog
version = attr: myapp.__version__
author = Ben Lopatin
author_email = ben@benlopatin.com
url = http://www.django-standalone-apps.com

[options]
packages = find:

[options.packages.find]
where = src
```

It's now possible to reduce your setup.py file to only the following, although the
setup.py file is still required by setuptools for building your package:

```
from setuptools import setup
setup()
```

This has added a file and some additional lines of code; however, the result is
arguably easier to understand, and with the affordances built into setuptools for reading
attributes for version and loading files (like your README) to populate description
fields, it's arguably a much simpler configuration format.

The pyproject.toml and more tooling

To close out this chapter, we're going to add yet another configuration file and then look
at using it as a total replacement for both setup.py and setup.cfg. PEP 518, "Specifying
Minimum Build System Requirements for Python Projects,"[2] specifies a top-level TOML
file that can be used to define which packages are required just to build the package in
question, that is, your standalone Django app.

---

[2]https://www.python.org/dev/peps/pep-0518/

> TOML, "Tom's Obvious, Minimal Language," is a specified,
> INI-like configuration language that allows nesting.

The pyproject.toml file is designed to be a top-level file with a PEP-specified format, one that is tool agnostic (contra setup.py) and also can be reused by various development tools for their configuration.

The example file in the documentation represents the base one would need to include: setuptools for building the package and wheel for building the wheel archives:

```
[build-system]
requires = ["setuptools", "wheel"]
```

However, PEP 518 also specifies a customizable (tool) header, wherein configuration can be added for various development tools, including build and testing (note that this support is entirely dependent on the tools themselves, too). This allows alternative build systems to use the pyproject.toml file as a source of build instructions and package metadata.

One such tool is Poetry, and by using it to build your Django standalone app – or any Python project – you can rely entirely on the pyproject.toml file without a setup.py or setup.cfg file. Here's a short example that includes the requisite package metadata and separate dependency definitions for building the project and for development. This precludes needing one or more pip requirements files, as well, because the dependency definitions are used to create a "lock" file with precisely pinned versions resolved by Poetry for version compatibility.

```
[build-system]
requires = ["poetry>=0.12"]
build-backend = "poetry.masonry.api"

[tool.poetry]
name = "myapp"
version = "2.5.0"
description = "Support for multi user accounts"
authors = ["Ben Lopatin <ben@benlopatin.com>"]
license = "MIT"
packages = [
    { include = "myapp", from = "src" },
]
```

```
[tool.poetry.dependencies]
python = "^3.5"
Django = "^3.0"

[tool.poetry.dev-dependencies]
pytest = "~5.0"
pytest-django = "~3.7.0"
```

The benefits of clarity, version management, and file consolidation make using a tool like Poetry a tempting alternative to using setup.py and setuptools. It is worth considering a few potential downsides however. There's no simple way to provide the version in one canonical source in your package, meaning you will need redundant version declarations. More complicated build procedures scripted with Python may not benefit from or lend themselves to a declarative configuration. And the project itself is still relatively new and driven largely by a single developer, meaning the "bus factor" of the project is quite small. That being said, as long as alternatives exist,[3] the lock-in cost is small.

Summary

In this chapter, you learned how to improve your experience packaging your standalone Django app by creating a single source for the package version to prevent errors due to duplication, by using a separate source directory to ensure that tests are run against the package as installed, and by relying on additional files like setup.cfg and pyproject.toml to build Python wheel packages and simplify build requirements.

In the next chapter, you will learn about licensing for your standalone app including what software licenses provide and how to include them.

---

[3]Including setuptools and Flit, another pyproject.toml centric build tool

PART IV

Managing Your Standalone App

CHAPTER 18

Licensing

As users of open source software, most developers probably take for granted the copyright and licensing conditions of the software we use. This is a little harder to do when you're distributing your own software. It may get further complicated if you need to include other software with your own.

> Author's note: Nothing in this chapter should be construed as legal advice. If you have legal concerns around licensing or using licensed software, you should seek professional legal advice.

What licenses do

The first thing that licenses do is explicitly state the copyright ownership of the software. In most jurisdictions around the world, copyright is granted merely by the act of creating a new work. Many countries provide means for registering copyrights, but this step is not necessary; copyright is automatic. Possessing copyright and asserting it are two different things however.

Second, licenses are an agreement. They are an agreement on terms between the creator of the software and the user. In the case of a web application, the user would be the developer or whoever is deploying the software (e.g., a business). The terms included are diverse, but the mechanism of agreement is most often *use* in one way or another of the software.

The terms of the license may be strict, such as those included in common commercial licenses. Some licenses may prohibit copying or redistributing the software, modifying it, or even using it in certain ways. Other licenses, like common open source licenses, may freely allow you to do whatever you want with the software just so long as you include the license with its copyright and terms. These terms consist of some combination of rights and obligations.

© Ben Lopatin 2020
B. Lopatin, *Django Standalone Apps*, https://doi.org/10.1007/978-1-4842-5632-9_18

At a basic level, the terms of most open source licenses deny any warranty or liability from the use of the software. It's provided for free with access to the source code, after all. This probably seems unnecessary especially in the context of a Django standalone app. However, given the close-to-zero cost of disclaiming any liability from something shared with unknown people in a potentially litigious society, it's not a bad step to take.

Beyond this though, it may seem unnecessary to declare any terms if your intent is to share your standalone app with the world for free (there are licenses just for that!). However, a key aspect of a license is the fact that it does explicitly allow anyone to do what they want with it. It means that someone else can't claim your software for themselves and then dictate different terms.

Varieties of licenses

There are a multitude of licenses in use today, but they fall into several categories:

1. Commercial licenses

2. Open source licenses

3. Public domain licenses

Commercial licenses are those enacted by and only by paying customers. Microsoft Windows and Apple macOS, for example, are commercial licensed software. These typically disallow any kind of modification or redistribution and more often than not come without any access to the source code.

Open source licenses are diverse, but are united in that they provide access to the source code. Most software licensed under open source licenses can be freely modified and redistributed, although the terms beyond this may vary significantly. These terms can broadly be further divided into two categories: (1) permissive and (2) copyleft.

> *A "permissive" license is simply a non-copyleft open source license — one that guarantees the freedoms to use, modify, and redistribute, but that permits proprietary derivative works.*
>
> —Open Source Initiative

Permissive licenses include the MIT, BSD, and Apache licenses. These licenses largely grant the user free right to use the software however they see fit. They can repackage it in a closed source and commercially licensed software distribution if they want. The only requirement is that they pass along your license.

> *"Copyleft" refers to licenses that allow derivative works but require them to use the same license as the original work.*
>
> —Open Source Initiative

Copyleft licenses include the variants of the GPL or GNU Public License. These licenses require not only that their license is passed along but that the terms of that license are applied to any other software that uses it. The key activator for copyleft licensing is modification of the source.

Public domain licenses are essentially anti-licenses. They make no assertion of any rights to the source code or on the ability to restrict how the source code is used. They also grant no rights or permissions and as such are not as practically attractive as they may be philosophically.

Which should you choose? The specific license you choose for your own project or projects is less important than (a) choosing one and including it in your standalone app and (b) choosing a preexisting license. The former will give other people the confidence that they can use and if need be modify your software. The latter ensures that you have a license that other people can understand and recognize.

How and where to include your license

There are several obvious places to include your license, depending on how much of the license you include in any given place. This can include

- The license identifier, for example, "MIT"
- The license summary
- The entire license

At a minimum you should include the entirety of the license and copyright notice in a top-level license file. This ensures that you check off every box, and this is an expected place to find it.

The next spot for your license is in your setup.py file, using the license argument to the setup() function to identify the license. This ensures that the information is immediately available on package indexes, in a highly visible and searchable way.

Where else might you want to include it?

- In you README, to at least identify the license at a glance

- In your root module, for example, __init__.py, using a dunder value such as __license__

- In your project documentation

- In the individual Python files themselves

As far as including the license in individual Python files, this is unnecessary. It's a common practice in enterprise-sponsored open source projects that makes it abundantly clear who owns the copyright and what the license entails. The primary benefit to any other developers is that it makes it easier for people using extracts of your code, for example, vendoring a single module, to include your copyright and your license.

How to include other licenses

In some cases you may want or need to directly include other preexisting software in your standalone app, whether this is "vendoring" an entire package or including only an individual module. If you do this, you must ensure first that predecessor license of that software allows this kind of distribution. Next you must ensure that the license with which you distribute your app is compatible with the predecessor license. And lastly you must include the predecessor license.

The first question is really whether or not the predecessor software has a license and whether it is an open source license. Whatever the license used, it should explicitly permit the redistribution and modification (if using only a part) of the software. The answer to this question will be fairly obvious if predecessor license is a common one, like an MIT or GPL license. For custom or "vanity" licenses, you may have to do a little bit of research.

The second question pertains to the specific rights and obligations granted and required by the predecessor license. Some licenses, like the MIT license, make no obligation for how the software is reused so long as the original license is included. Others, like variants of the GPL, obligate any redistribution to be licensed in the same way. As such if you wanted to license your standalone app using the GPL and include some software that was MIT licensed, this would be feasible, provided of course you made clear which components were covered by which license. On the other hand, if you wanted to license your standalone app using the MIT license, you would not be able to include GPL-licensed software in your distribution. To be clear, this does not mean your app *cannot use software with incompatible licensed packages*, only that you cannot include the software in what you distribute. Reuse through installable packages is fine.

The third and final question is how to include the predecessor license. Even if the predecessor software uses the same license as your app, you must still include predecessor license. This captures more than just the terms of software license, but copyright ownership, too. A good place to start is your top-level license file. Here you can append to your own the copyright notice of the predecessor software in reference to the components that it pertains to. In many cases, this will be sufficient.

If you're using an individual module, you should include the license or at least an abbreviated reference to it directly in the module. Using code comments is a fine idea for this purpose; using a module docstring may confuse *how to* documentation with license notice.

```
# -*- coding: utf-8 -*-
# COPYRIGHT (c) Some Other Developer
# This source code is licensed under the MIT license found in the
# LICENSE file in the root directory of package.
```

For shorter licenses, it's customary to reiterate the entirety of the license in such a comment, but you need not do this provided you include the license and make the reference obvious. If you're vendoring a package, including the entirety of it, you can rely on the inclusion of licensing in the modules themselves and, notwithstanding that, include the original license file to the package directory for inclusion.

Summary

In this chapter, we reviewed what software licenses are and what they do, both for you and for the users of your standalone app. We also examined some of the options available to you as a software author for licensing app, the tradeoffs involved, how to approach licensing when including other software, and some sensible strategies for including the license information itself in your standalone app.

In the next chapter, we'll learn about releasing new versions of your app, what's required in this process, and how to streamline it.

CHAPTER 19

Documenting your standalone app

Once you've released your standalone app to the world, someone else will want to use it. How will they use it? How will they install it? And does it solve the same kind of problem they have? In this chapter, we'll look at how you can start addressing the challenge of documenting your standalone app.

Starting with questions

Regardless of what formats and tools you use to document your standalone app, or how you decide to distribute documentation throughout your codebase, all of your documentation should be motivated by answering the questions that someone else – even future you – will have when approaching your standalone app.

Several of the questions you should ask are *who will be reading this* and *what are they trying to do*. Most often the "who" will be a developer user, someone who is either assessing whether to use your standalone app or looking for help in integrating it into their project. But it may also be someone else, another project stakeholder trying to assess whether your standalone app should be considered one of the project options.

The "what" someone is trying to do is more important and more straightforward to break down. Let's categorize these questions as follows:

1. Is this standalone app a good fit for my project?

2. How do I start using it?

3. What is it fully capable of doing?

4. How can I report a bug or get involved?

© Ben Lopatin 2020
B. Lopatin, *Django Standalone Apps*, https://doi.org/10.1007/978-1-4842-5632-9_19

The first question is about *assessment*. By assessment I don't mean ranking or scoring your app for some kind of arbitrary scale, but judging whether someone should use it. This is the broadest and most subjective kind of questioning someone will have looking at your standalone app, and there is no single, surefire way of addressing this question.

However, there are several critical questions you can and should address that go a long way toward helping people assess your app, including (i) answering what problem it solves, (ii) how it solves that problem, and/or (iii) how it solves this problem differently from other solutions.

A concise example of this is from the standalone app django-rq:

> *Django integration with RQ, a Redis-based Python queuing library.*
> *Django-RQ is a simple app that allows you to configure your*
> *queues in Django's settings.py and easily use them in your project.*

We now know exactly what this is for and what it does. We don't know how to install it or use it yet, but from only those two sentences, you'll probably have a fairly good idea as to whether this app will be of help to you.

Once someone has decided to use your app, they'll next want to know how to start using it. This includes (i) installation, (ii) configuration, and (iii) any subsequent integration or usage steps.

Installation is typically straightforward, including a pip install and adding the app to INSTALLED_APPS, but you should be sure to make explicit the names used here and document any differences from the expected. As to configuration, at a minimum you'll need to include any changes or additions to project settings (beyond INSTALLED_APPS) that are required, such as MIDDLEWARE additions, and also additions to the project urls.py configuration.

Integration and usage include changes to the user's own code required to make use of your standalone app and any commands or output that the user should know about. If your standalone app includes mixin classes for views, what attributes or methods should the user be aware of immediately? If it includes management commands, what are they named and what are the required arguments? There is much more you can include, but for immediate answers, questions like this will guide what to include.

Lastly are the questions of how a user can provide feedback or contribute back to the project. It's easy to take these questions for granted and to think that the answers are self-evident – just create a new issue on the repo of course! – but that's not always the case and you should make this clear for your users. A simple statement about where to file issues or whether there is an email for asking questions suffices as a start, but you can and should include more guidance, including not just where to record issues but how. This will save your users time and you as well.

The forms of documentation

Documentation should start with a README file. This is a single, top-level text file with or without basic markup formatting (e.g., README.rst or README.md). It describes what your app does and how to install it and configure your project to use it and either includes some basic usage documentation or points to where that can be found. This file is typically the first thing someone will see when they see your app in a public repository, and it's easy to include the content here in the long_description used by setuptools to include in PyPI. It's also a long-running convention, so regardless where you include the rest of your docs or how you structure them, someone can expect to find this file at the source root.

Beyond this it helps to start your documentation in either separate files or sections in a way that address the hierarchy of needs in using your app (Figure 19-1).

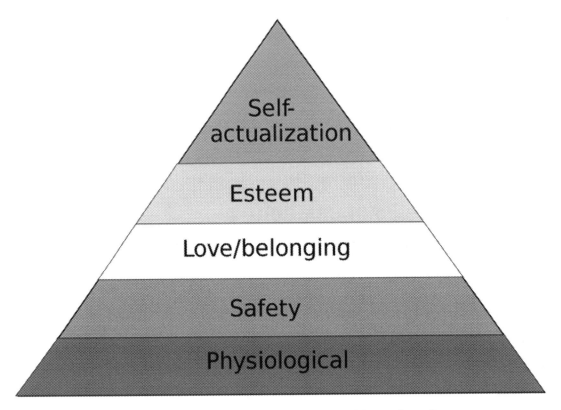

Figure 19-1. *Maslow's hierarchy of needs, illustrated by Wikipedia user FireflySixtySeven (CC BY-SA 4.0)*

This hierarchy of needs mimics Maslow's popular hierarchy of needs, which is intended to illustrate a hierarchy of human needs, whereby the lowest level must be satisfied before those above can be met. Whether or not the psychological theory is true, it's a useful analogue for approaching documentation.

At the base level come **installation and configuration**. Without knowing how to actually get your app and what "dials" need to be turned, all the subsequent documentation is of little practical value. Often the README itself will suffice for this purpose, but if the available settings are more than a few, then installation and configuration, or just configuration, may warrant their own section in the documentation.

Subsequent to this is the basic usage and integration described in the preceding section. A handy way to think about this is getting started with your app quickly, and a **quickstart** is an excellent way of showing how to make practical use of your app without needing to dive into the full documentation. This is usually the bare minimum required to start using the app, from the most commonly used command to a simple practical example integrating your app into another.

For apps that require non-trivial integration, such as building blocks or even additional frameworks, a **tutorial** on doing so is a valuable next step. A tutorial guides the user through the steps of using software by example with a clearly defined end goal that each step helps achieve. This won't be necessary for many standalone apps, but for apps with significant features, it is useful for showing how to use the app where a quickstart is insufficient.

As an example, the django-graphene app, a standalone app for adding GraphQL functionality to Django project, uses two such tutorials in its documentation. The basic tutorial guides the user through the typical quickstart steps and then proceeds through creating example models and views in a sample app and even loading provided test data to match the prescribed models. From here the user can actually see how the app works by building a small app and compare the results described in the documentation to the results they see on their own computer.

Whereas tutorials provide a "horizontal" approach to documenting a standalone app by starting with a problem whose example solution includes many different aspects of functionality, **API references** provide a "vertical" source of documentation, with details that are organized by implementation. The Django docs are largely organized this way. Rather than including tutorials for every type of problem, the Django docs include a basic tutorial and then detailed documentation organized logically by functionality. There is no tutorial on how to create an app that sends out aggregated book ranking information in email reports, but there is detailed documentation about how to use email, how to use Django's model classes, and about the various database aggregates and expressions.

Lastly, and at the top of our hierarchy, sits the **cookbook**. As might be expected from the name, cookbook documentation is a collection of recipes, of small real-world examples, that both demonstrate how to use the features of your standalone app and provide a measure of inspiration for how it can be applied. These can be extracted from real use cases or contrived, though they should be useful whether made up or not.

Code comments and docstrings

Many Python programmers are careful to document their code, including comments for "interesting" code blocks; detailed docstrings explaining modules, classes, and functions; and even type hints. Clearly written and well-documented *code* is a fantastic aid for development, especially for new contributors, and can be an asset for developer users who simply want to better understand the internals of your app. That said, there is a difference between code documentation and *usage* documentation.

The reasons why include not just how one reads the documentation (see the section "Tools for documentation") but organization and level of detail. Simply put, source code isn't typically organized to answer the questions of *why* and *how* when those questions have to do with the problem the app is solving; it's organized to solve the problem. The entry points are designed for execution and importing, not for reading and browsing. There's also value in decoupling documentation from source code when that separation makes contributing to the documentation easier.

Be wise about not mistaking code documentation for user or project documentation.

Tools for documentation

Once you have documentation for your standalone app, the next step is to make it readable for potential users without needing to look through source code. Whether you have used reStructuredText or Markdown, there are several tools that will make turning your documentation into web deployable HTML a snap.

The most commonly used tool for this is Sphinx, which is designed primarily for working with reStructuredText documentation, although it does have support for Markdown as well. If you've ever read either the Python or Django documentation, you've read through documentation generated by Sphinx. It is a powerful tool, but getting started is straightforward. To install it and create your initial configuration, run the following commands in your console from within your docs source directory:

```
pip install Sphinx
sphinx-quickstart
```

The sphinx-quickstart command will guide you through several prompts to help identify where to include the built HTML, basic project information, and the natural language in which docs will be written. The generated Makefile – or make.bat if you're using Windows – can then be used to read your reStructuredText source files and create browsable and searchable HTML files. You can also build to other formats, including PDF, though this may require additional software, such as LaTeX.

The details of structuring your documentation using Sphinx and reStructuredText are beyond the scope of our discussion here; however, reStructuredText allows you to create rich indexes and also build documentation from your standalone app's source code.

An alternative to Sphinx for those who strongly prefer using Markdown is MkDocs. What Markdown and MkDocs lack in features, they make up for in simplicity. MkDocs projects are configured using Yaml files instead of Python, and Markdown's syntax – as well as features – are more stripped down compared to reStructuredText. This can be an asset if you're working with other people who are already familiar with Markdown. Just like Sphinx, MkDocs will take your documentation source and create browsable, searchable HTML documentation.

Once you have a tool that can turn documentation source into HTML, you're nearly ready to deploy it so that developer users can browse the documentation online. The simplest way to do this is to simply provide the built HTML over the Web, for example, copying it to a web server, adding to a repository branch to serve using GitHub pages, among others. While this works, it does introduce a lot of manual work.

Instead, you can use Read the Docs to automatically build and host your project documentation. Read the Docs will work with either Sphinx or MkDocs, and provided you are using GitHub, Bitbucket, or GitLab, it will allow you to connect your repository using a project integration to build from repository updates (you can use it with other source code platforms too; however, it will require more manual setup).

Summary

In this chapter, you've learned how to get started with user-facing documentation for your standalone app, including what kind of questions to ask in guiding it, forms of documentation suitable for users, and tools for actually deploying documentation.

In the next chapter, we'll delve into additional topics in testing including testing migrations and how to test against different versions of Python and Django.

CHAPTER 20

Additional Testing

Once you have your standalone app successfully tested outside of your project, it might seem like you're entirely done with testing. However, there's quite a bit more than you can test for and guard against, which becomes especially important as more people use your app and decide to contribute.

In this chapter, you'll learn how to test for bugs that aren't caught by typical unit tests, how to test against multiple versions of Python and Django, and the pytest test framework as an alternative to the Django test runner.

Testing migrations

There are a few aspects of your database migrations that you may wish to test, including the schema changes themselves, the accuracy of data migrations, and whether you have any unmigrated changes.

For testing the schema migrations, it should suffice to have tests in place for your models. You typically don't need any special tests for these changes. In the event your migrations include non-trivial data migrations, you may wish to test that these populate or modify app data as expected. If this is the case, you'll want to test the specific migration or the migration function itself (i.e., the code run by `operations.RunPython` in the migration file). If you're testing the full migration as a complete unit, this necessitates managing the migration flow, which can be accomplished with a modified TestCase class or by using a purpose-built library such as `django-test-migrations`. In the event the data migration uses concrete models – which is generally considered an anti-pattern because of the lack of point in time model attributes – you can often treat the individual migrating function as a unit and test directly. This involves setting up some test data as expected in the initial phase, executing the migration function, and verifying that the data in the test database now matches the expected result.

© Ben Lopatin 2020
B. Lopatin, *Django Standalone Apps*, https://doi.org/10.1007/978-1-4842-5632-9_20

When it comes to unmigrated changes, what we want to discover is if there are any outstanding model changes that would result in a new database migration and treat this scenario as an error. There are two reasons to do this. The first is that you risk shipping what is effectively an incomplete model state. If you've changed the allowed states of a model field, for instance, such that it can no longer be nullable, and your test data fill this field, then you may not notice that the migration is missing, leading to a problem when someone else deploys an updated version of the app. The second reason is that you will end up shipping the app in a state where end users running makemigrations make their own new migration for your app, which is likely to conflict with subsequent migrations that ship with your app (I have done this myself and it proved very annoying!).

Related to both of these reasons, it's entirely possible that you have all the necessary migrations but accidentally fail to commit them to your source control repository. As a result your tests will pass locally, but you'll ship it in a broken state. Having tests in place means that you can tests for missing migrations in a continuous integration system that only works with what you've committed and pushed.

Testing against different versions

More exciting and important than testing migrations is being able to sensibly test against multiple versions of both Python and Django. There are several reasons to test against different versions of Python and Django. Most obviously, if you're publishing your standalone app for other people to use, you simply cannot assume that everyone else is using the same version of either Python or Django. For every single version of Django your app supports, there is a set of supported Python versions which that version of Django will run on. There can be no *guarantee* that an app or library supporting a given Django version also supports all of the associated Python versions; however, it is a very reasonable expectation that it will support all of the associated versions.

Secondly, testing against multiple versions of Python and Django makes the job of future proofing your app much easier. You can continue building versions that support your current chosen environments while ensuring compatibility with new versions of Python and Django, even before they're officially released.

There are several tools that will let you do this, including continuous integration services and local tools like tox and nox. We previously covered how to use tox in Chapter 15. nox is a *somewhat* similar tool, in that like tox it will create, manage, and use individual test-specific virtual environments for running your tests. However, unlike tox it uses a Python-based configuration. This allows you to do things like chain "sessions", the task related blocks nox lets you write to run tests and other tasks.

Here is a fully functional nox configuration file (noxfile.py) extracted from a work-in-progress branch from django-organizations:

```
import nox

pytest = '4.4.1'

@nox.session(python=['3.6'])
@nox.parametrize('django', ['1.11', '2.0'])
def tests(session, django):
    session.install(f'pytest=={pytest}')
    session.install(f'Django=={django}')
    session.install('-r', 'requirements-test.txt')
    session.install('-e', '.')
    session.run('pytest')
```

Why use nox instead of tox? The primary reason would be personal preference for composable Python-based configuration rather than an ini file-like configuration format. A more compelling reason would be the ability to use it to both run tests and execute non-test commands, like building or publishing, thus consolidating the use cases for tox and a Makefile.

Using pytest

Django uses the Python standard library's unittest test framework by default. The bundled TestCase classes are based on unittest.TestCase and the test runner at root is too. However, the unittest library is not the only way to test Python code, and one alternative which has grown increasingly popular is pytest.

pytest has a few primary advantages over the unittest library for writing and running tests. The first is that pytest lets you write tests using individual functions without needing to create whole classes. Second, pytest makes use of the built-in assert statement for comparisons, so there is no need to make use of methods like assertEqual. For example, given this form class

```
from django import forms
from dateutil.relativedelta import relativedelta

class AgeValidity(forms.Form):
        birthdate = forms.DateField()

        def clean_birthdate(self):
                dob = self.cleaned_data["birthdate"]
                if dob + relativedelta(years=18) < date.today()
                        raise forms.ValidationError("Min. age not met")
                return dob
```

you can write a basic validation check in a single function:

```
import datetime
from dateutil.relativedelta import relativedelta

def test_form_date_validity():
        given_date = date.today() - relativedelta(years=18, days=-1)
        form = AgeValidity(data={"birthdate": given_date})
        assert not form.is_valid()
```

It's a simple test, of course, but it doesn't require anything more than what would be the test method in a test class, however a test class doesn't need to be written. By themselves these features are conveniences. Rather, it is the combination of composable test fixtures, test running, and the plugin ecosystem which make it a compelling alternative.

Instead of creating instances of test data in setUp or setUpTestData of each TestCase class, you can create individual and reusable functions that return (or yield) your test data. pytest then matches these with test function argument names and passes the data through, without requiring an explicit import statement. Here are two pytest fixtures – generators that yield test data – including one that relies on the other.

```
@pytest.fixture
def account_user():
    yield User.objects.create(
                username="183jkjd", email="akjdkj@kjdk.com")
```

```
@pytest.fixture
def account_account(account_user):
    vendor = create_organization(
                account_user, "Acme", org_model=Account)
    yield vendor
```

These can then be used in any test by naming the arguments to match the fixtures:

```
def test_invite_returns_invitation(
        account_user,
        account_account,
):
        backend = ModelInvitation(org_model=Account)
        invitation = backend.invite_by_email(
                "bob@newuser.com",
                user=account_user,
                organization=account_account)
    assert isinstance(invitation, OrganizationInvitationBase)
```

The accumulated benefit over your test suite is less setup and teardown through the tests and less effort spent creating the requisite test data.

In order to use pytest like this to test your standalone app, you'll most likely need to use the pytest-django plugin. This makes interaction with the database a snap and comes with some fixtures (or fixture generators, if you want to think of them that way) for typical Django-related testing, like a test client for accessing views. Using pytest-django to mark a test as having access to the database, here is a pytest test function for verifying that there are no uncreated migrations:

```
@pytest.mark.django_db
def test_no_missing_migrations():
    call_command("makemigrations", check=True, dry_run=True)
```

There are reasons not to use pytest. For one, your unittest-based test suite may be working just fine for you. The implicit loading of fixtures during test runs is convenient but can obfuscate where fixtures were sourced from, and the magic of this feature may be unappealing. However, for small standalone apps, it can make it easier to start writing tests, and for very large standalone apps, it can make it easier to reuse test data and run unique, feature-specific sets of tests.

Summary

In this chapter, you've learned about verifying migrations during testing, tools for testing against different versions of Python and Django, and using pytest as an alternative test framework. In the next chapter, we'll tie this all together through automation, adding both local and remotely executed processes which simplify the development process for you and provide a good foundation for enabling other developers to contribute as well.

CHAPTER 21

Automating

In the previous chapter, we extended what you can do to test your standalone app by testing against different versions of Python and Django, as well as alternative test runners. You learned how to use tox or nox to test against different versions and how to test your migrations and got a brief introduction to the pytest testing framework.

In this chapter, we'll look at how to go beyond this by automating as much as possible, not merely for our convenience but also to help improve the quality of our app and the shared experience for other contributing developers.

What is it and why bother?

There are a number of ways you can define automation, but for our purposes, we'll start with this definition: *it's any process that sequences other processes without requiring subsequent intervention.* Our emphasis here on some kind of parent process is because *something* or *someone* still needs to kick off the process, and moreover, automation is not something that's only satisfied by robots or some kind of cloud-based system. Test automation, after all, can be executed by running a command on your own computer. What makes it automated is that the entirety of the test suite can be run with just that one command.

So if "automation" sounds daunting, start by substituting "scripting" and you'll get 80% of the benefit.

The first reason to start automating is that you're likely to have to do these things again, and you want to ensure that you do them exactly the same way every time. You don't want to forget a step; you don't want to have to wait at the keyboard to kick off the next step.

Less obviously, it saves time and mental energy from thinking about the tasks you automate. You likely want a certain outcome, and even knowing that doing X will get you Y, if it's easy to skip X, you likely will. Much like staying healthy, your best bet is

© Ben Lopatin 2020
B. Lopatin, *Django Standalone Apps*, https://doi.org/10.1007/978-1-4842-5632-9_21

making enforceable decisions ahead of time. Automating is a way of not just ensuring better outcomes but spending fewer mental cycles on the work required to achieve those outcomes.

Automating development processes also makes it much easier to get other people involved. Should you simply hope that everyone will follow the same steps when testing their code and creating pull requests? Are you going to make them follow steps in documentation and copy and paste like code monkeys? Of course not! You can give them a single script that automates all the steps they need to follow to do the same thing you did. And better than this, if you set up a separate service, you don't even need to rely on contributors running these tasks themselves. This saves onboarding time, debugging time, and stress.

Starting to automate

There are a number of different *things* you can start automating, including tests, related code checks, the release process, and also different *places* you can start automating, for example, locally or using remote processes. Absent an urgent and specific need, you should start automating (i) critical tasks that would be blockers for release or even further deployment, like tests, (ii) development-related tasks that make it easier for other developers to participate, and (iii) later tasks related to release that make life easier and can reduce the short-term bus-factor.

Testing is the most straightforward to automate because you *already have tests* that you can run. Once you have usable and useful tests, it's helpful to have them run automatically, for example, every time you push code to your repository. This ensures that the tests are always run, whether you remember to run them locally or not. This is a little fringe benefit if you're working on your own, but it's a benefit that scales up with each additional developer. You no longer need to worry if someone else ran the tests before pushing up their code or submitting a pull request, you can see the results for yourself.

Continuous integration services

The foundation of most automation is a continuous integration service. This is a service – whether a self-managed process like Jenkins or a third-party SaaS – that runs specified tasks for your project. These can include, and most often do, running the test suite and reporting the results, as well as deploying updates, and can be run in response to updates to the codebase or triggered from some other action.

Here we cover a few of the more popular third-party services, with basic configurations for a standalone app that requires only Django and uses a runtests.py file to kick off the tests. These can be used as starters, but more importantly, in combination their commonalities describe at a high level how these services work.

Travis CI

Travis CI is the granddaddy of continuous integration as a service, at least for open source software. Using this service requires a configuration file, named .travis.yml, in the root of your project and following your project on GitHub through the Travis web app. The Travis service only supports GitHub-based projects.

A simple test set up is extremely simple:

```
os: linux
dist: bionic
language: python
python:
  - "3.8"

install:
  - pip install django==3.0
script:
  - python runtests.py
```

Beyond this, Travis offers good support of version matrixing (similar to tox), natively supporting running tests against multiple versions of Python concurrently.

GitHub

GitHub has long been the most popular choice for hosting open source software projects with Git. More recently GitHub added their "Actions" feature which allows running various workflows on a per project basis. These are added with individual YAML files in the .github/worflows/ directory of your project.

An example to achieve the same test run as the Travis example is as follows:

```
name: Blog
on: [push]
jobs:
  build:
    runs-on: ubuntu-latest
    steps:
      - uses: actions/checkout@v1

      - name: Set up Python 3.8
        uses: actions/setup-python@v1
        with:
          python-version: 3.8

      - name: Install dependencies
        run: |
          pip install Django==3.0

      - name: Run the tests
        run: |
          python runtests.py
```

The GitHub Actions test job configuration here is more verbose than the Travis configuration, in large part because GitHub Actions is not a continuous integration per se, but a generic workflow building tool on which you can compose your own required continuous integration tasks. This makes it more flexible but a bit more complicated. The primary benefit of using GitHub Actions for most people is simply that for projects already hosted with GitHub, it's immediately available without any further integration.

GitLab

GitLab is another Git-hosting service and an alternative to GitHub that integrates a CI product directly into both the web app and the installable self-hosted version, which is open source:

```
image: "python:3.8"

before_script:
  - pip install django==3.0

stages:
  - Test

test:
  stage: Test
  script:
  - python runtests.py
```

GitLab's CI service is purpose built, and as such a basic configuration is simple. However, it is highly customizable and unlike the other CI-as-a-service products is open source and can be self-managed.

CircleCI

CircleCI is in the business of continuous integration, and like Travis they offer various options for free and paid plans available for open source projects. A brief example of a test workflow looks like this:

```
version: 2
jobs:
  build:
    docker:
      - image: circleci/python:3.8.0

    working_directory: ~/repo

    steps:
      - checkout

      - run:
          name: install dependencies
          command: |
            python3 -m venv venv
            . venv/bin/activate
            pip install django==3.0
```

```
- run:
    name: run tests
    command: |
        . venv/bin/activate
        python runtests.py
```

Others

This is hardly an exhaustive list of services or software you can use to automate testing your standalone app.

Summary

In this chapter, you have learned how to take advantage of automation systems to make it easier to test your code, to test it in different environments, and to provide an authoritative test oracle for your app. Each of these steps serves to reduce friction in the development process for both the original author and subsequent contributors. In the next chapters, we'll look at when to use database-specific functionality in your app and how to encourage collaboration on your standalone app from other developers.

## CHAPTER 22

Databases and other backend-specific considerations

One of the benefits of using a framework like Django is that it provides abstracted interfaces to differing *backend services*, ranging from databases to email and caching. A typical deployed Django project only needs to support one, or maybe two, of any given database or backend, and this lends itself to using backend-specific features within individual projects. These features may grant additional functionality or performance benefits, but in a published standalone app will limit the app's usage to only uses of the specific database or backend.

In this chapter, we'll briefly but separately review questions about using specific database choices in your app, including when to include backend-specific features and how to approach them when you do.

Backend-specific implementation and features

One of the benefits of using an ORM like Django's is that it is database *agnostic*. The same application code can be run using PostgreSQL, MySQL, or even SQLite. Yet there are times when it may seem, or indeed be, advantageous to use database-specific functionality. Beyond the commonalities, each database works differently, offers slightly different functionality, and has different strengths and weaknesses. If you know what database your project is going to use, it makes sense to take full advantage of those specifics.

© Ben Lopatin 2020
B. Lopatin, *Django Standalone Apps*, https://doi.org/10.1007/978-1-4842-5632-9_22

We should note here that an overall assumption to this question is that your standalone app is intended for a broader audience. If your standalone app is for internal use only within a larger organization using a common technology stack, this is going to be less important.

The most straightforward example of database-specific code is that of raw SQL. Putting aside whether it's a good idea to ship raw SQL in a deployed project, the typical benefit of using straight SQL is that you can directly rely on database features, including database functions, which have not been exposed in the ORM. You can often also write more expressive queries on a one-off basis.

However, the ORM is database agnostic; even Django ships with database-specific features! The contrib.postgres app includes PostgreSQL-specific database functions, fields like RangeField and ArrayField, indexes, and full-text search functionality that isn't available (in Django) for other databases.

Approaching database-specific functionality

As a rule of thumb, unless your app is specifically focused on some kind of database or backend-specific functionality, try to avoid relying on those database or backend-specific features unless absolutely needed.

An obvious candidate for relying on backend-specific functionality is geospatial functionality. GeoDjango, that is, contrib.gis, supports multiple database backends; however, only PostgreSQL's PostGIS is fully feature supported. The model fields can be used across the supported database backends; however, a number of lookups and functions are supported inconsistently by the different geospatial database backends. If in fact there's significant value in using one of these, such as geospatial aggregates or bounding box overlaps, then this is a fair use of backend-specific (or backend-limiting) functionality.

There are workarounds for this, of course, to include database-specific functionality without limiting the scope of use for developer users. One is including the functionality without directly integrating it into some other critical functionality, for example, adding a query method that relies on backend-specific functionality but not using it in a provided view or admin class. A further benefit to your developer users would be to include warnings if their database backend does not support the given features, or if it is unknown if it does (any custom backend classes may obscure this to your code).

```
import warnings
from django.conf import settings

if (
        'django.contrib.gis.db.backends.postgis' not in
        [db['ENGINE'] for db in settings.DATABASES.values()]
):
        warnings.warn("""PostGIS not found, not all App features
                    may be supported.""")
```

A bolder approach which will work in some cases is to back out of the backend-specific functionality altogether. There are two ways of approaching this: (i) using a simpler implementation and (ii) allowing developer users to integrate their own classes (using inversion of control). The first strategy will work in limited cases, and a proven geospatial example is storing geospatial data such as coordinates or even polygons. If your app makes no use of this data for lookups or geospatial querying and does not present a clear use case for doing this, non-geospatial fields will suffice. Coordinates can be stored in a pair of fields using DecimalField and access with a property.

```
class Place(models.Model):
        latitude = models.DecimalField(...)
        longitude = models.DecimalField(...)

        @property
        def coords(self):
                return self.latitude, self.longitude

        @coords.setter
        def coords(self, lat, lng):
                self.latitude, self.longitude = lat, lng
```

Polygons are a bit tougher, but again, if the data is only being stored or represented in another layer, for example, provided via an API for a front-end application to render, then its storage requirements are less specific. An ArrayField might suffice (though also be PostgreSQL limiting) or a JSONField could as well (now supported by MySQL in Django 3).

An alternative where some kind of backend-specific feature is needed is to allow some component class to be registered or used as an initializing argument that adheres to a baseline interface but can otherwise be wholly controlled by the end user. The way Django's database backends works meets this requirement, as do similar features in other projects like Haystack, for search. In either case you provide the library with the dotted path to the backend class or module using Django settings, and the library loads and uses that specific class or module. This means the backends are infinitely customizable (or nearly so), allowing users to swap between different search engines and also to create modified versions that suit their specific needs whether those needs are small features or working with a new and totally different backing service.

Summary

In this chapter, you've learned about various types of *backend-specific* options and how to judge whether using them is a good strategy for your standalone app.

## CHAPTER 23

Collaborating

Open source software tends to imply – though it doesn't *necessitate* – collaboration with other developers, often strangers from around the world. Our previous chapters have largely been predicated on the idea that you will be publishing and sharing your source code with the world. This is such standard practice that we rarely think about *why* we'd do this and what the benefits and costs might be, to say nothing about how to achieve them.

Collaboration can be a challenge, but it's one that's almost always worthwhile. In this chapter, we'll look at how you can expect people to collaborate, your role as a maintainer, and some strategies to maximize the effectiveness of those contributions and to minimize the burdens of open source maintenance.

Why contributions

It's a good idea to start with laying a framework for answering "why" to allow and foster collaboration on your projects and also to understand why other people seek to contribute in one way or another to your projects.

As the maintainer the expected or desired benefits from contribution include:

1. Identifying bugs

2. Updating documentation

3. Suggesting features

4. Developing features

Regardless of the type of contribution, the common thread behind most contributions is a desire to use your software. A user may report a bug because they just want to help out and make the software better (improving an otherwise fruitful experience), or because it's something they want fixed so they can start or continue using the software (fixing a blocking bug). Someone suggesting a feature probably wants to see

B. Lopatin, *Django Standalone Apps*, https://doi.org/10.1007/978-1-4842-5632-9_23

that feature in your app because they are using or want to use your app, and that feature would further improve it (for them, at least!).

Similar reasons for authoring and maintaining an open source project can be found in contributing, too. It's not just a desire to help others, but a desire to improve their own technology solutions and sometimes to see their suggestions triumph as well. Vanity should always be considered in open source software!

We can summarize by stating that the three motivations for contributions will be some combination of a pure desire to help or make right (altruism), a desire to improve the product for their own use (practicality), and at times a desire to see their own suggestions take flight (vanity).

What to expect

The most common forms of contribution are not fully tested, well-documented pull requests that satisfy a proposed feature or even solve an outstanding bug. The most common forms of contribution will be bug reports and feature requests. Moreover, many bug reports will simply be questions (some even answered in documentation). In part, these are the easiest forms of "contribution" to a project with the lowest barriers to entry.

Regardless of what's contributed to your project, you'll need to understand that there are benefits as well as costs to allowing and inviting other people to collaborate with you. It takes time to review and respond to issues and to pull requests, and it can require emotional energy to manage other peoples' expectations and even, occasionally, demands! Sometimes even well-intentioned people will forget or fail to realize that the project is run by other human beings, more often than not of their own good will and on their own time.

So whatever you can do to minimize the friction for all parties involved will tend to not only improve the quality of collaboration but also your life as a maintainer.

Setting expectations

There are two strategies to take in combination to help contributors add to your project while minimizing the extra work required of you. The first is automation (discussed already in Chapter 24) and the second is being abundantly clear and upfront about how collaborators are expected to contribute and what to expect from you in turn.

The benefits of automation from locally run scripts to server run tests and deployment processes are several fold. A significant benefit is that where tests and checks are run by a continuous integration service, you don't need to check and run the tests yourself locally to verify new code. Yet another one with a more social angle is that having an automated *oracle* for some decisions reduces the decision-making burden from you and also the focus of blame if the contributor might disagree or otherwise feel threatened by a decision. Some simple examples include code formatting and coverage. If you have automated checks for these things, even though you've set them up, if someone's contribution fails them, you don't need to say "I'm not accepting this because I did or looked at X and it's not good enough", you can simply say "Ah, once you get the thing passing over there, we can merge it in." The rule codified in automation is less likely to suffer any anger and you have fewer decisions to make and communicate.

There will always be significant aspects of the collaboration process that cannot be automated though, and in a similar vein, these can be solved or improved through clearly documenting expectations. This will not only make your life easier but make it easier for contributors and typically improve the quality of their contributions.

The first place to start with is a contribution guideline, often included as a top-level standalone file like CONTRIBUTING.rst. Whether this is a standalone file or included in your readme is less important than what it includes. Here you have the opportunity to express to potential users what the best channels of communication are, where they should report bugs, what information should be included when reporting bugs, and even what to expect from you or other maintainers after they report a bug.

Depending on what code publishing service you use (e.g., GitHub, GitLab), you can create templates from which collaborating users can make a report or request. The benefit of a template is that you can ask upfront for the kind of information you'd need to start assessing what the issue is. A simple issue template for a GitHub-based project might look like the following,[1] which would prompt the reporter for the required debugging information:

Bug reports:

Please replace this line with a brief summary of your issue **AND** the following information:

---

[1]Based on public domain issues from https://github.com/stevemao/github-issue-templates/ blob/master/checklist/ISSUE_TEMPLATE.md

- [ ] 1. Python version:
- [ ] 2. Django version:
- [ ] 3. MyApp version:
- [ ] 4. Reproducible test code (if feasible/relevant):

Features:

Please note by far the quickest way to get a new feature is to file a Pull Request.

We will consider your request, but it may be closed if it's something we're not actively planning to work on.

The same kind of template can be replicated for pull requests as well[2]:

Types of changes
<!--- What types of changes does your code introduce? Put an `x` in all the boxes that apply: -->

- [ ] Bug fix (non-breaking change which fixes an issue).
- [ ] New feature (non-breaking change which adds functionality).
- [ ] Breaking change (fix or feature that would cause existing
      functionality to change).
- [ ] I have read the **CONTRIBUTING** document.
- [ ] My code follows the code style of this project.
- [ ] My change requires a change to the documentation.
- [ ] I have updated the documentation accordingly.
- [ ] I have added tests to cover my changes.
- [ ] All new and existing tests passed.

This allows a submitter to check off what they represent was done, making explicit and upfront what's expected, making your review easier, and also delegating to a policy the decision making and possible requests for updates. However, if you look through the pull request template, you'll note at least a few items that could be further delegated to automated scripts, for example, verifying that all tests pass and, to a reasonable extent, that the code matches the desired project style.

---

[2]Also from the GitHub issues template repository

Another feature to aid documentation that you might consider is a *code of conduct*. At its simplest, a code of conduct is an expectations document, stating upfront how people collaborating on the project are expected to work and communicate together. These have become more popular largely in response to toxic or hostile behavior that can be manifested in open source collaboration. However, even if you're not actively worried about trolls, a code of conduct is something that can be delegated to instead of perceived ad hoc decisions.

The role and obligations of an open source maintainer

What is the role of the maintainer? How should you define your obligations both to users and to contributors? These are *intentionally* goading questions that share some popular assumptions about the "job" of a maintainer. The short answer is that both questions are ultimately up to you to decide.

The role of the maintainer is to answer questions and shepherd development, and this will vary largely based on how active development is on your project, including how many other contributors are involved. If there are active contributors and development, you may turn your role largely into that of a traffic cop, pointing people in the right direction and stopping them from getting into accidents. Or you may be the primary author for all subsequent updates.

The question of obligation is trickier. It's of less direct impact to the processes you use and more critical simply for your own well-being. When you choose to publish and release open source software for free, people will use it. Subsequently, even well-intentioned users and contributors may make requests or demands of the project maintainers that they feel you are obligated to fulfill. This can range from issuing new releases to adding new requested features. These can be overwhelming for big projects with high adoption, and even small projects at the wrong time can be beleaguering for maintainers.

The key to answering the question of your obligation is the tension between taking responsibility for the things we share for use and the fact that your users and your contributors are using free (as in "free beer") software. Every subsidiary question rests on the latter fact, and because of this, any obligation you have to issue new releases or develop new features is solely of your own construction and your freedom to dispense with.

What this ultimately means is taking care to be upfront and transparent about both the state of your published Django app and the state of known issues. It may be the case that your app isn't production ready or that a particular bug is going to take more time to resolve than you currently have. You do not have an obligation to make your app production ready on anyone else's schedule or to fix the bug – really. You don't even have an *obligation* to tell anyone when you will, though a good faith effort in communicating about that goes a long way toward building good will among current and potential contributors.

Ultimately our free, open source software is given freely. The code can be assessed and it can be modified for one's own use, and barring a transaction in which you explicitly require some kind of payment from your users, the old adage *caveat emptor*, "let the buyer beware," is the core obligation.

Summary

In this chapter, you've learned about the ways in which potential contributors will want to collaborate on your project, as well as some strategies for encouraging high-value and effective collaboration. This includes communicating how to make different kinds of contributions as well as how to envision your relationship to the project and users to avoid feeling overwhelmed.

In the next chapter, we'll take a brief tour of how to use app templates for creating Django standalone apps.

CHAPTER 24

Using app templates

Once you've got the hang of creating your own standalone apps, you might want to start writing more. At this point you'll likely find there are a number of decisions you don't want to make over and over again and necessary boilerplate that you don't want to deal with writing. One solution to this is to start creating apps from templates.

In this chapter, we'll review some of the options for creating new standalone apps from templates, including Django's own startapp management command for starting new apps and the venerable Cookiecutter tool.

startapp

You've probably read about and used Django's startapp management command to create new apps within your own Django projects:

```
./manage.py startapp myapp
```

By default this command will take an app name and create a directory with minimal file structure, including models.py and tests.py files, based on a templates directory structure in the Django package:

```
myapp/
        migrations/
        __init__.py
        admin.py
        app.py
        models.py
        tests.py
        views.py
```

© Ben Lopatin 2020
B. Lopatin, *Django Standalone Apps*, https://doi.org/10.1007/978-1-4842-5632-9_24

The core functionality of the command is described for creating apps within the context of an existing project. However, there is no reason the command cannot be used to create the app structure anywhere else; simply use the django-admin script instead:

```
django-admin startapp myapp
```

By itself this isn't terribly useful, as the only benefit is a small collection of all-but-blank files created in a specific directory. This can be improved by creating and using your own template directory and providing this an argument to the startapp command using the --template flag, for example:

```
django-admin.py startapp myapp --template ~/app.template
```

By using your own template, you can not only choose different files to use, you can pre-populate them with common imports and other code you use. The startapp command has support for a few specific context variables, including the app name, so you can also include some app-specific references in these files. Moreover, you can change the entire structure, including the app as a package within a parent directory with your setup files, README, among others.

This strategy will likely suffice if you're creating apps based on the exact same structure and feature set each time. However, the minimally supported template context means that even with templating support, there's little room for configurability.

Cookiecutter

For a more robust alternative, consider using Cookiecutter. Cookiecutter is a Python package described as "A command-line utility that creates projects from cookiecutters (project templates)." Using a combination of Jinja templates and a cookiecutter JSON configuration file, you can create highly configurable projects based on a single cookiecutter from an interactive prompt.

After installation using pip, brew on macOS, or apt-get on Debian, creating a project from a remote template is a single command:

```
cookiecutter https://location.com/of-the-cookiecutter.git
```

> It's worth noting that while Cookiecutter is a Python package and is widely used in the Python community, cookiecutter project templates can be created and used for any kind of project, irrespective of the language.

Perhaps more significant than the feature set provided by Cookiecutter is the community of publicly shared cookiecutter project templates, including templates for creating both "vanilla" Python packages and Django standalone apps. The benefit of using a community-built template is several fold, including eliminating the time and sundry decisions required to create a template from scratch, as well as getting a number of best practices "for free" which have been vetted by numerous users.

The primary downside is less that a template might exclude some feature that you want and more that they might be overly complex and feature rich for your needs. It may be more effort to edit than to start from scratch. In the case of the most popular Django package cookiecutter, pydanny/cookiecutter-djangopackage, there aren't many overly specific decisions included, meaning it's a safe starting point that won't add unneeded cruft. It will enforce a top-level package (as opposed to using a source directory) and the specific Python and Django versions may not be quite up to date. Thankfully you can change these things. Figure 24-1 provides an example of the prompt provided by pydanny/cookiecutter-djangopackage for configuring a new Django standalone app.

```
full_name [Your full name here]: Ben Lopatin
email [you@example.com]: ben@benlopatin.com
github_username [yourname]: bennylope
project_name [Django Package]: Enterprise Class Twitter Clone
repo_name [dj-package]: enterprise_twitter
app_name [enterprise_twitter]:
app_config_name [EnterpriseTwitterConfig]:
project_short_description [Your project description goes here]: Tweets for the enterprise!
models [Comma-separated list of models]: Tweet,Like,Image,Link
django_versions [1.11,2.1]: 3.0
version [0.1.0]:
create_example_project [N]: y
Select open_source_license:
1 - MIT
2 - BSD
3 - ISCL
4 - Apache Software License 2.0
5 - Not open source
Choose from 1, 2, 3, 4, 5 [1]: █
```

Figure 24-1. *Prompt provided by pydanny/cookiecutter-djangopackage*

There are two ways to create your own cookiecutter project template for starting Django standalone apps: from scratch or by adapting an existing project template. Adapting an existing cookiecutter is as simple as cloning the source repository, making the requisite changes, and using your local clone as the template.

```
cookiecutter path/to/local/cookiecutter
```

Adapting an existing template means you don't have to start everything from scratch, from figuring out templated names for files to deciding how to track various package dependencies. If the changes you need are too radical, you can always start from scratch. When starting from scratch, keep in mind that despite the vast value of templating, the core of a template is copying files from one source to another. In other words, create your structure with as little configuration as possible to start and build up the configurability only as you need.

Summary

In this chapter, we looked at two ways of creating new Django standalone apps from templates: using Django's startapp command and the general-purpose project templating tool Cookiecutter. Both can be used with custom starting templates to enforce project design decisions for subsequent Django standalone apps; however, Cookiecutter's templating is more flexible than startapp and should be given first consideration as a standalone app templating solution.

Index

A

Admin–specific functionality, 38
Automation
    continuous integration
        service, 146–150
    definition, 145
    development processes, 146
    migration, 27–28
    starting, 146
    testing, 28–29, 146

B

Backend classes, 67
Backend-specific implementation
    application code, 151
    database agnostic, 152
    functionality or performance
        benefits, 151
blog_app directory, 46
boo_tags.py file, 12
Business feature *vs.* technical
    foundation, 55
Business logic, 105

C

CircleCI, 149
Code of conduct, 159

Collaboration

Collaboration
    automation, 157
    bug reports, 156
    cod od conduct, 159
    contribution, 155, 156
    GitHub-based project, 157
    open source maintainer, 159, 160
    template, 158
Continuous integration (CI) system, 9
Cookiecutter
    benefit, 163
    cloning, 164
    command-line utility, 162
    package dependencies, 164
    remote template, 162
    top-level package, 163
Copyleft licenses, 127
Currencies values, 13, 14

D, E

database_forwards method, 65
Database migrations
    guidelines, 29
    outside project, 27
    testing, 28, 29
Database-specific functionality
    approach, 153
    ArrayField, 153
    component class, 154

© Ben Lopatin 2020
B. Lopatin, *Django Standalone Apps*, https://doi.org/10.1007/978-1-4842-5632-9

Printed in the United States
By Bookmasters